"I have long believed that a solid und[...] psychological issues arises from soun[...] theology. In this book, Bill Perkins offers biblical perspectives to matters like control, pride, forgiveness, and respect. He shows how a mastery of such underlying issues will directly affect your use of anger. I like that. I like that a lot. If you follow the principles outlined in this book and seriously ponder the questions posed, you will be ten steps ahead of the rest of the crowd."

— **DR. LES CARTER**
Author of The Anger Trap

"Bill Perkins is a master storyteller. This is one of the most entertaining books for men I've ever read. I'd recommend it to any man who's dealing with anger."

— **DAVID MURROW**
Author of Why Men Hate Going to Church

"Bill has done it again. With psychological insight, biblical wisdom, and practical common sense, he has written a handbook, centered around seven riveting stories, to help us guys see past our defensiveness about anger and become the sort of men God wants us to be. From beginning to end, *When Good Men Get Angry* will challenge you with truths that will change your life, making you a better husband, father, and friend."

— **DR. STEVE STEPHENS**
Author of 20 Rules and Tools for a Great Marriage

"Bill Perkins offers godly wisdom dispensed with humor, candor, and straight talk. More important, he shows us how, through understanding our new identity in Christ, we can be mighty men whose anger is used as a force for good, not destruction. Powerful stuff!"

— **DR. DAVID HAWKINS**
Director of The Marriage Recovery Center
Author of 90 Days to a Fantastic Marriage *and* Dealing with the CrazyMakers in Your Life

WHEN GOOD MEN GET ANGRY

THE SPIRITUAL ART
OF MANAGING ANGER

BILL PERKINS

TYNDALE™
MOMENTUM

An Imprint of
Tyndale House Publishers, Inc.

Visit Tyndale online at www.tyndale.com.

Visit Tyndale Momentum online at www.tyndalemomentum.com.

TYNDALE and Tyndale's quill logo are registered trademarks of Tyndale House Publishers, Inc. *Tyndale Momentum* and the Tyndale Momentum logo are trademarks of Tyndale House Publishers, Inc. Tyndale Momentum is an imprint of Tyndale House Publishers, Inc.

When Good Men Get Angry: The Spiritual Art of Managing Anger

Designed by Dan Farrell

Library of Congress Cataloging-in-Publication Data

Perkins, Bill, date.
  When good men get angry / Bill Perkins.
    p. cm.
  Includes bibliographical references.
  ISBN 978-1-4143-1141-8 (hc)
1. Christian men—Religious life.   2. Anger—Religious aspects—Christianity.
I. Title.
  BV4528.2.P49 2009
  248.8′42—dc22   2009006404

ISBN 978-1-4143-6001-0 (sc)

Printed in the United States of America

20 19 18 17 16
8   7   6   5   4   3

|||

THE WIND AND THE WILLOW

I know
it sounds blue,
but still
it's true.
I spoke with a willow tree today.

"Why so sad, Miss Willow?" I asked.

"I long for my love," said she.

"Your love," said I.
"And what does he bring?"

"Why he's
strong,
and free,
and gentle,
and swift.
And sometimes he's terrible too."

"If you must know, my love is the wind.
For he swings my arms and I dance,
he tickles my leaves making me laugh,
when he strokes my fingers I sing.
He is all that brings joy to my soul."

"I now understand my own love," said I.
"And I also know something of yours."

"You know of the wind?" she asked in surprise.

"Indeed, I now realize.
He blows so you'll dance.
He breathes so you'll laugh.
He huffs and he puffs so you'll sing.
Without you, Miss Willow,
the wind has no song,
no dance
nor a light-hearted laugh.
You see, Miss Willow,
you are to the wind
all that he is to you."[1]

---

[1]Taken from my *Undiscovered Love Poems*

CONTENTS

INTRODUCTION

He who is slow to anger has great understanding.
—PROVERBS 14:29, NASB

MY CELL PHONE vibrated. I flipped it open, placed it to my ear, and said hello.

"Bill, it's Kevin. You won't believe what I've done. I need to come over . . . like now!"

"What's so urgent?"

"I'll be there in five minutes," he said. The phone went dead.

I've met few men with more fascinating life stories than Kevin's. He grew up in Seattle and ran away from home when he was fifteen. While sitting in a diner in Lake Union, the ship-building area of Seattle, he met the captain of an Alaskan fishing boat. When the captain realized Kevin had no intention of returning home, he invited him to join his crew. Without a moment's hesitation Kevin moved to the village of Oak Harbor on Kodiak Island—250 miles southwest of Anchorage. During the next two summers he worked on fishing boats; he attended school the rest of the time. After graduating from high school, he joined the Marines.

While Kevin looked like Robert De Niro, unlike the actor he didn't have to pretend to be tough. He had the size, speed, and meanness to do serious damage to anyone crazy enough to take him on. And whether it was because he started trouble or attracted it, Kevin got in a lot of fights.

And then his life changed. During the end of his military service a friend told him about Christ, and he became a devoted follower. When he was discharged from the Marines, he started his own business in Portland, Oregon.

As I pondered Kevin's story, I figured he was about to tell me another outlandish tale. The doorbell rang. I opened it, and Kevin stepped in—not waiting for an invitation.

"What's so urgent that it couldn't wait?" I asked.

"I just got in a fight," he said as we entered my office. "I could have gotten in serious trouble."

"What happened?"

"I was driving my pickup south on 205 when three guys in a souped-up black Trans Am sped past me. The driver tossed a Coke can out his window, hitting my windshield and splattering it with Coke. He and his friends looked at me and laughed. I laughed too and acted like it was a big joke. I slowly eased past them and pulled into their lane. When they were right behind me, I slammed on my brakes.

"The guy almost rear-ended me. If they had just figured we were even it would have ended there, but they signaled me to pull over. I followed them onto the shoulder of the road. I guess they thought they were tough guys. The driver jumped out of the car, pumped up his chest, stomped over to me, and took a swing with his right hand. But I blocked his punch and hit him with three quick jabs that bloodied his nose. When his friends realized someone would get hurt—and it might be them and their friend—they broke it up."

I stared at Kevin, dumbfounded. "Kevin, you're thirty-five years old. You've got a wife and two kids. What were you thinking?"

"I guess I wasn't thinking," he said.

"Do you feel better now that you've punished the guy?"

"No. I feel terrible. I could have hurt someone and ended up in jail. Besides, I've got that 'I Love Jesus' bumper sticker on my back fender, and the guy in the Trans Am almost wiped it off. I wasn't the best example."

For years Kevin had bridled his anger and avoided such idiotic conflicts. And then a single event triggered the beast within. He didn't rein it in until it was almost too late.

Kevin's story illustrates the kind of foolish and harmful decisions some men can make when angry. Of course, most guys don't resort to physical violence when they're mad. More men use sarcasm, the withdrawal of affection, or verbal debates to express their anger. Amazingly, a small percentage of men deny they ever get annoyed or angry. I suspect that a handful of men call anger another name, like frustration or excitement. Or it may be they view anger as such a terrible evil that they refuse to admit it's an emotion they experience.

Regardless of how often you get angry or how you express it, I've written this book to provide you with both the insight and the biblical strategy you need to process and express your anger in a healthy way. When I wrote this book I didn't have in mind men like Bruce Banner, who morphs into the Incredible Hulk when he gets angry. Instead, it's written for ordinary men who occasionally hurt people when they lose their cool. It's for men who want to manage their anger in a godly way.

3 percent of surveyed men said they never get annoyed by what other people say or do.

80 percent say they get annoyed a few times a day.

15 percent say they get annoyed many times a day.

One percent say they're annoyed all the time.

This book has two parts. In the first, I'll take you inside anger so you can discover some foundational truths: what it is, where it comes from, how Jesus expressed anger, and why I'm confident the new and good man in you can learn to control it.

The second part of the book deals with the six issues I think are crucial to understanding, processing, and expressing your anger in a godly way. The six issues are:

Identity
Respect
Control
Pride
Forgiveness
Blessing

Each of these issues is fleshed out with stories of men who have successfully battled their anger. All of the stories are based on actual events, although I've changed some details and added fictional material to disguise the men's identities. Also, I've placed each situation within the context of counseling sessions as a way to better illustrate how anger is often exhibited and rationalized, as well as how it can be addressed and effectively managed.

After I had written the book I realized, with advice from the editorial team at Tyndale and some women who had read the manuscript, that a chapter was needed to help women encourage their husbands or boyfriends as these men learn to process and express their anger in a godly way. I hope your wife or girlfriend will read the entire book so she'll better understand you. But the final chapter is written specifically with her in mind.

Throughout the introduction and chapters 1 through 8, you'll find italicized statistical information that I derived from surveys I e-mailed to almost five thousand men. These men receive my weekly e-mail and live across the United States. I surveyed them to determine what makes men angry and how they respond when angry. I have included their responses in the book because I think they will provide you with a gauge to see how you compare with other men.

The response to the different surveys was varied, but the sampling was substantial. And while the surveys are not scientific, I think they provide a reliable reading of the men who took them. The questions were developed with the assistance of a licensed psychologist, and the data was analyzed by James C. Hassinger, an operations research and systems analyst in Saint Charles, Missouri.

The data for the statistics in chapter 9, the one written for women, was derived from almost three hundred women who responded to a survey sent to over 3,700 households via the Internet.

In order to help you think through the issues that surface in each chapter or talk about them with other men who are reading the book, I've provided discussion questions at the end of each chapter. You'll also find a summary of each chapter under the heading "Truths to Live By." Because I think Scripture meditation is crucial to internalizing what you'll learn, I've provided you with a few key verses under the heading "Strengthen the Good Man."

As I wrote this book I thought repeatedly about the words of Solomon in Proverbs 16:32:

> *He who is slow to anger is better than the mighty,*
> *And he who rules his spirit, than he who captures*
> *a city.* (NASB)

I pray as you read this book God will make you:

slow to anger;
better than the mighty;
ruler of your spirit;
better than those who capture a city.

I'm convinced my prayer will be answered because the four statements above describe the new and true you—who you are in Christ. The rest of the book will help you understand this new identity and discover how good men process and express their anger.

PART ONE

INSIDE ANGER

CHAPTER I

GETTING AT THE CORE OF ANGER

As a boy I loved starting fires. And by the time I was only eight years old, I had become adept at it—though getting my hands on matches or my mom's cigarette lighter required great cunning since my parents didn't leave them lying around. And once my parents realized they had a "fire bug" living in their home, they kept them hidden.

I started my most impressive fire in a vacant lot across the street from our home on Juniper Street in Roswell, New Mexico. What prompted me to light the fire was a pile of debris that someone had dumped in the middle of the lot. This was no trash can full of garbage but a sizeable truckload of paper, tin cans, paint buckets, planks of wood, and other junk.

Every day my dad complained about the pile of trash. He even called the city and forcefully demanded they clean up the mess. But nobody lifted a finger or a foot to remove the rubbish.

My eight-year-old mind heard the garbage heap calling to me like the sea nymphs of ancient Greek mythology whose sweet singing lured mariners to their destruction on the rocks surrounding their island. Of course, I didn't know about Greek mythology at age eight, but that pile of rubbish seemed to be begging me to use it as fuel for a fire.

One day my mom left me under the supervision of an older sister. When my sister's friend called and asked if she could come over, I urged her to leave, promising to behave. Once she was gone, I grabbed the five-gallon gas can from the garage. With the focus of a superhero out to save the world, I carried the can of gas over to the rubbish pile and doused some of the paper, wood, and other junk with the fuel. I then lit a match, tossed it on the gasoline, and ran back to my house, where I called the fire department.

*69 percent of surveyed men said that
as children they lit fires without adult
supervision just for the fun of it.*

A few minutes later the red fire truck, its siren screaming and red lights flashing, raced down Juniper Street. Curious neighbors formed a small crowd as the firefighters hooked up a hose to a fire hydrant and began spraying the flames with a powerful torrent of water.

Once the fire had bowed to the will of the water and turned into steam and smoke, I casually approached a firefighter and asked, "How do you think it got started?"

He looked down at my freckled, angelic face, rubbed his chin with his right hand, shook his head, and said, "Don't know for sure. Probably spontaneous combustion."

In that moment I felt a surge of pleasure because my misdeed had gone undetected and I saw my neighbors gazing at the remaining puffs of smoke with the wonder of children at the zoo. I felt even more joy a few days later when the city sent out a crew to clean up the mess.

MY FINAL FIRE

That experience inspired me to plan an even more daring blaze later in the year. Behind our house ran a dirt-and-gravel alley that a sanitation company drove down to pick up garbage left in aluminum trash cans. During the spring and summer, Mini Cooper–sized tumbleweeds grew just behind our four-foot-high white wooden fence, which lined the alley.

I didn't know much about gas meters, but since the one for our home rested under the tumbleweeds, I figured I might trigger an explosion. I waited until late in the summer when the tumbleweeds were as dry and flammable as gunpowder. I then crammed some crinkly old newspapers under their branches, being careful not to scratch my hands or arms on the tiny needles that ran up and down the tumbleweed spines. Adrenaline raced through my body as I quickly swept the wooden match across the sandpaper edge of the matchbox. The tiny flame appeared and quickly exhaled a small puff of sulfur-smelling smoke. I heard a dog bark in the alley to my right and thought I had been caught. But when I looked up he wasn't in sight, so I held the match to the bottom edge of the paper. With a sudden *swoosh*, an orange fireball jumped higher than the fence.

Surprised, I backed to the other side of the alley, as unaware of the danger as a moth inspecting a lit candle. Meanwhile, inside the house my mother was washing dishes at the kitchen sink. When she looked out the window she saw the flames shooting into the air just behind the fence. I heard her yelling as she raced out the door, turned on the water spigot, grabbed the garden hose, and ran toward the fire. I watched in stunned silence as she quickly put out the fire before it could ignite the fence or cause a gas explosion.

In less than a minute she had undone all of my plotting and planning. She had doused my dreams of flammable fun. If she had simply nodded an acknowledgment of my presence and respectfully said, "Boys will be boys, but you must be more careful," I would have been disappointed but not mad. But since she was my mother she felt a responsibility to discipline my misdeed. And so with the quickness of a cat after a rat she grabbed me by the right wrist and pulled me across the yard, up the back porch, and into the kitchen. "I'm going to give you a spanking you'll never forget!" she screamed.

Looking back I realize I should have lowered my head and said nothing. But the tighter she squeezed, the harder she dragged, and the louder she yelled, the madder I got. Of course, my mother's threat didn't concern me. Because I had learned that she lacked the will or the strength to hurt me, I said, "Go ahead and spank me. Please, Mother, spank me as hard as you can. I want you to." I then bent over and patted my rear with my right hand, indicating where I wanted her to spank me.

68 percent of men surveyed considered their relationships with their mothers to be good or excellent.

At that precise moment I heard a sound behind me that caused me to lose my breath—as though I were being held underwater and drowning. I turned my head and saw my dad standing behind me. He had heard my outrageous outburst of boyish anger and disrespect.

As a boy I adored my dad. He played catch with me, taught me to ride a horse, and told me amazing stories about his childhood. At the time I saw only his strengths and none of his weaknesses. And while he never disciplined me in anger—and he didn't appear angry on this particular day—I had a healthy fear of what I knew he would do because of how I had spoken to my mother.

"So you want a spanking?" he asked. I realized it wasn't a question but a reminder of what I had just told my mother.

"No, Dad. I don't! I was kidding . . . just kidding." I pleaded with my dad not to spank me. I promised never to do anything else wrong if he would just forgive me this one mistake.

86 percent of surveyed men
were spanked by their dads.

79 percent were spanked by their mothers.

70 percent said they would rather
have their mothers spank them.

My dad, a man with Popeye arms, took off his belt and made a loop with one end in each hand. "I promise you, when I'm done you'll never talk to your mother like that again, no matter how mad you get." And he was right. After that well-deserved and memorable experience, and the conversation that followed, he had cured me of starting malicious fires *and* talking to my mother like that.

THREE CORE ISSUES

Do you think if I had known my dad was standing behind me I would have expressed my anger differently? When I'm speaking before a men's group and ask them that question, the crowd usually responds with a round of laughter—the answer is that obvious.

And then after a long pause, I ask them, "So the issue of anger management boils down to my relationship with my heavenly Father, doesn't it? If I live with an awareness of his presence, I can and will control what I say and how I act when I'm angry. Not because I fear him in an unhealthy way, but because I want to please him and know he won't shield me from the consequences of my sinful choices."

Since that's the case, why don't we, as Christian men, control our anger?

I think there are three core issues that we must address. First, we must learn to understand our new and true identity in Christ. Second, we must live with an ongoing awareness of the presence of God. Third, we must understand the source of our anger and how we can process and express it in a healthy way that accomplishes good and not harm.

I realize those three statements may seem like an oversimplification of a complex matter. And, yes, understanding, processing, and expressing anger in a healthy way involves tangled and complex issues. But these three issues make up the core of the problem and its solution.

At the moment you became a believer, you became a new man in Christ. (I discuss this more extensively in chapter 3.) This *new you* is your *true* identity. Even as a believer, however, you still possess the flesh—that part of you that craves gratification apart from Christ. Whenever you allow your flesh, with its unbridled anger, to control your thinking and drive your behavior, you've suffered the worst kind of identity theft. You're no longer acting in accordance with the new and true identity you have through Christ, but you're allowing your flesh, with its destructive anger, to define how you think and act.

94 percent of surveyed men said they would like to know how to process and express their anger in a godly way.

From your childhood, the flesh has dug a deep channel of thoughts, feelings, and actions that direct your response when you're angry. When something triggers your anger, you probably react, not from your new and true identity, but from the flesh. You may even think that you have no choice in the matter.

This book is written to help the good man in you—the man who is being transformed into the image of Christ, the man who possesses God's Spirit—learn how to process and express your anger in a way that's consistent with your true identity in Christ. And I'm certain if you put into practice what you'll learn in the following pages, you'll live like the good man you are—even when you get angry.

TRUTHS TO LIVE BY

- As I understand my new and true identity in Christ, I will think and act more like Jesus.
- As I live with an awareness of God's presence, I'll control how I process and express my anger.

- I can learn how to use my anger in a way that accomplishes good and not harm.

STRENGTHEN THE GOOD MAN

When I am raised to life again, you will know that I am in my
Father, and you are in me, and I am in you. (JOHN 14:20)
I have loved you even as the Father has loved me. Remain in my
love. (JOHN 15:9)
I am certain that God, who began the good work within you,
will continue his work until it is finally finished on the day
when Christ Jesus returns. (PHILIPPIANS 1:6)

DISCUSSION QUESTIONS

1. When you were a child, did you ever get into trouble because of a bad behavior, such as lighting fires?

2. As a child, how did you express anger?

3. How do you express your anger now?

4. What sorts of things make you angry?

5. How would an awareness of God's presence affect the way you deal with your anger?

6. How can you cultivate that awareness?

7. How do you hope this book will help you?

CHAPTER 2

AN ALIEN EXPERIENCE

My childhood hometown is best known for the Roswell Incident, the crash of a mysterious craft in the desert north of the city on July 8, 1947. The military orchestrated a secretive cleanup, explaining they had been called in to collect pieces from a top-secret surveillance balloon that crashed. Other eyewitnesses insisted the debris came from an alien spacecraft. Though I wasn't born until two years after the Roswell Incident, I grew up knowing about this strange event that put our small city on the map and became a pop culture phenomenon.

So you can understand what my wife meant when she once told me, "I think that UFO deposited an egg that hatched two years later. That would explain your . . . umm . . . strangeness." It also explains a bizarre daydream I had.

In the dream I'm standing in the middle of a remote and barren field, surrounded by rocks and tumbleweeds, in the middle of nowhere, outside Roswell. As I gaze at the dry earth where the alien spacecraft crashed, I see a rift in the ground. I *know* instinctively that a single alien survived the crash. And I also know he managed to store a pod in that fiddle-shaped fissure just before he died. And I realize it is the place of my hatching.

As I stand there I'm suddenly enveloped by a bright beam of light. I fall to the ground, like a puppet whose strings have been cut.

Hours later I wake up under several tumbleweeds—the same size as the ones that grew in the alley of my boyhood home in Roswell—which have blown over me. In my hands rests a two-hundred-page book that weighs less than a pound and carries the title *Understanding Your Alien Identity*.

I brush aside the tumbleweeds, sit up, and thumb through the pages of the book. In this moment I know I'll spend the remainder of my life studying this volume, which, fortunately for me and the world, is written in English and not an alien script. I'm sure its pages will explain the secret of my alien powers and tell me how I can use them for the good of mankind.

THE KEY TO ANGER MANAGEMENT

I snap out of the world of fantasy and consider what I've been dreaming about. I realize that since such stories are the stuff of science fiction, most people ignore all references to alien life on our planet. Yet, as a follower of Christ, I am an alien. According to the *American Heritage Dictionary*, an alien is "A person from another and very different family, people, or place."[1] As a follower of Christ, I have a different family, and my home is in a different place. Yet my alien identity wasn't derived from some make-believe extraterrestrial, nor is it described by an alien document left outside Roswell. Instead my alien identity came from God and is described in the pages of the Bible.

Paul said I became a new creation with a new identity in Christ when God gave me his Spirit (2 Corinthians 5:17). Peter told his readers that they were "aliens and strangers" (1 Peter 2:11, NIV) and that they had an "inheritance" that is kept for them in heaven (1 Peter 1:4). Paul told the Philippians that they were "citizens of heaven" (Philippians 3:20).

It's a spiritual reality that if you've trusted Christ as your Savior:

> you're an alien who is visiting this world;
> you're a stranger here;
> you're truly a new man, a good man in Christ.[2]

This truth, which seems as strange as science fiction, is the truth about you. And it's *the key* to managing your anger.

WHY BEGIN HERE?

Before I go deeper into the subject of your new identity, you may wonder why I would start a book on anger with a chapter that focuses on your true and new identity in Christ. After all, most books on anger begin by exposing the seriousness of the problem. They tell you it's not healthy to yell at your wife, kids, and coworkers. It's not good to cut people down to size with sarcasm, humor, or your debating skills; to freeze them out with the silent treatment; to drive like a maniac; or to whine all the time and blame others for your problems. I don't mean that you do *all* of those things when you're mad, but it's a list my research tells me characterizes angry men. And there's a good chance one or more of those behaviors describes an angry you.

I suspect you already know you need to learn to bridle your anger or acknowledge and express it in a healthy way (or someone you care for needs to). If you require convincing, this is the wrong book. If it's the right book, and I hope it is, then we can get right to the heart of the issue.

58 percent of men surveyed say their anger
and how they've expressed it has hurt a
relationship with a family member or friend.

I begin here because I believe the key to successfully processing and managing your anger rests in your new identity as a Christian. Ultimately, when any of us fail to deal with our anger in a godly way, we've allowed our flesh, that part of our personality that seeks gratification apart from God, to steal our identity. We then think and act consistently with our sinful and self-serving passions. We must recognize when this is happening and choose to act in a manner that flows from our new life in Christ instead. But for that to happen, we must first understand our new identity.

The problem we often encounter with anger is that it is such a powerful emotion, like a raging river, that we go with the flow, unaware that we can slow it down or divert it in a constructive direction.

Yet managing anger involves mentally disengaging from our emotions and thinking. And such reasoned thinking is something most of us lack the training and discipline to do when we're angry. Ultimately, what we think, either good or bad, about ourselves and the actions of others creates the energy that drives our anger. And only correct thinking will enable us to harness its power and steer it in a safe and constructive direction.

I think anger and sex are similar in that both are powerful forces that energize a man and have the potential for good or evil. And while many Christian men have sought to bridle their sexual thoughts and actions, they have not done so with their anger. I think it's because many men view anger as a wild beast that can't be controlled, so they make little effort to do so. When it runs away with them on its back, they just go along for the ride—even when they're heading for a cliff, which should scare them stiff, but doesn't. Or they may bridle anger at work but let it run wild at home, trampling their wives and children under its bone-hard hooves.

I want you to know that you can control your anger. By God's grace, this powerful emotion that has caused you and those you love such grief can be used for good and for God's glory.

WHAT IS ANGER?

Anger, according to the dictionary, is an intense emotional state induced by displeasure.[3] Obviously, though, something has to trigger this rush of emotion—like the guy who cuts us off on the freeway. Immediately as he pulls in front of us, our temperature rises, our adrenaline surges, our heart rate increases, and our blood pressure spikes. Without much thought, we might camp on the horn or race ahead and cut the other driver off.

Anger never discriminates; it involves the entire person—body, mind, emotions, and will.

Despite the damage it can do, destructive anger is the distortion of something good. In his book *The Other Side of Love*, Gary Chapman notes that, while anger is not an essential part of God's nature, it flows "from two aspects of God's divine nature: God's holiness and God's love."[4] When he sees the harm that results from man's sin, God gets mad. In fact, the word *anger* is used 455 times in the Old Testament, and in 375 of those instances God is the angry one. Chapman explains: "It is God's concern for justice and righteousness (both of which grow out of His holiness and His love) that stimulate God's anger. Thus when God sees evil, God experiences anger. Anger is His logical response to injustice or unrighteousness."[5]

> God created us in his image, so it's logical
> that we also have a concern for justice
> and righteousness. "Anger, then, is the
> emotion that arises whenever we encounter
> what we perceive to be wrong."[6]

The problem is we often get mad about *perceived* and not *actual* wrongs, or we react to a level-one wrong as though it were a level-ten wrong. Jesus never did.[7]

WHEN JESUS GOT MAD

When we look at Jesus, we find that even when wronged, he seldom got angry. And when he did get angry, he moderated how he expressed it. Four instances when he got mad stand out to me—the two cleansings of the Temple at the beginning and end of his ministry (John 2:13-25; Matthew 21:12-17), the time when the disciples prevented the children from coming to him (Mark 10:14), and the Sabbath when the religious leaders indicated it was unlawful for him to heal on that day (Mark 3:1-5).

The Greek word used in Mark 10:14 indicates that Jesus felt "indignation" toward the disciples. When Mark describes how Jesus looked at the Pharisees with anger, he uses a different word, *orge*, which refers to anger as the strongest of all passions.[8] Clearly, Jesus felt intense anger toward the hard-hearted Pharisees. In that same verse, however, Mark notes that he felt "sympathy" or "grief" for them as well.

When you're mad, how often do you feel compassion for the person you think wronged you? If you're like me, that happens about as often as you express gratitude to a police officer who pulls you over for speeding.

No doubt Jesus' compassion tempered his anger—he genuinely understood and cared for the people who repeatedly disrespected and injured others.[9]

And how about when he cleansed the Temple? While his actions were aggressive, they were appropriate for the situation. Remember, Jesus was thirty years old when he first cleansed the Temple. He had probably visited the Temple during every Passover celebration since he was twelve, each time hearing the cacophony of mooing, bleating, and shouting that accompanied the calls of the merchants and money changers.

Because the only "clean" money was Jewish money, people with foreign currency had to exchange it before buying overpriced animals to present as an offering to God. But what may have most stoked Christ's anger was that all of this happened in the Court of the Gentiles—the only place where non-Jews could come to pray and worship God. Instead of creating a quiet place of prayer, the Jews had turned it into a loud and smelly marketplace.

I suspect that each time Jesus entered the Court of the Gentiles the scene fueled his fire. When he finally expressed his indignation, he fully understood the injustice suffered by the worshipers and the disrespect shown to his Father's house.

As Jesus entered the Temple that day, he grabbed pieces of rope, loose tethers, and baggage-cords and began plaiting them into a rope. Then, without warning, "gentle Jesus, meek and mild" turned into a tornado of activity. The disciples' eyes must have popped wide open when Jesus swung the whip, driving out cattle, sheep, oxen, *and* their owners from the busy courtyard. Then he poured out the coins of the money changers, flipped over their tables, and forced the stunned men to make a quick exit. To those selling doves, he said, "Get these out of here! How dare you turn my Father's house into a market!" (John 2:16, NIV).

I recently spoke at a men's conference and said that we were to follow the example of Jesus in the processing and expressing of anger. A few days later I received a scathing e-mail from a pastor who said, "We're to follow Jesus in his humility. Not in his anger!"

Yet I think Jesus expressed his anger with humility. And I'm convinced we're to follow his example in everything. After all, Jesus never lost control of himself. He wasn't in the grip of anger. Instead, he kept anger in his grip. In fact, he demonstrated restraint by not releasing the doves in the Temple courts. If any of the other animals had been set free, they could be rounded up and the money recollected. But if Jesus had released the doves they would have flown away, causing loss to their owners.[10]

Now here's the cool part: you and I are capable of processing and expressing our anger just as Jesus did his. This truth rests on the fact that as his followers he lives in us and we live in him.

As I noted before, and will mention again, our new and true identity is in him. Just as a page finds its identity in a book or a letter of the alphabet finds its identity in a word, so we find ours in Jesus Christ.

I begin this book by pointing you to Jesus because he is the solution to your anger issues. He is the example for you to follow, the healer of your soul, and the bridle for your rage.

I'm persuaded that a mature Christian man is one who understands his true identity in Christ and lives according to that identity. (I'll talk about your true identity in the next chapter.) The more you understand who you truly are, the more you'll act in harmony with your new and true nature. For that to happen you first need to realize how your flesh (or "old man," as some Bible translations refer to it) has shaped how you see yourself and how you act—especially how you process and express anger. And then you'll need to get a glimpse of your true self in Christ. So take some time and review what you've learned in this chapter. Talk it over with a friend. And then when you're ready to move on, begin reading part 2.

TRUTHS TO LIVE BY

- The spiritual reality is that I'm an alien, a stranger on the earth, and a good man in Christ.
- My anger is one indication that I'm made in God's image.
- Jesus models for me how to wed compassion with anger.
- I can learn to process and express my anger in a healthy way, just as Jesus did while on earth.
- When I process and express my anger like Jesus did, God will use my passion to advance his Kingdom.

STRENGTHEN THE GOOD MAN

But we are citizens of heaven, where the Lord Jesus Christ lives.
And we are eagerly waiting for him to return as our Savior.
(PHILIPPIANS 3:20)

And because you belong to him, the power of the life-giving
Spirit has freed you from the power of sin that leads to death.
(ROMANS 8:2)

This means that anyone who belongs to Christ has become
a new person. The old life is gone; a new life has begun!
(2 CORINTHIANS 5:17)

DISCUSSION QUESTIONS

1. Why is it important to stress your new identity in Christ as a way of helping you manage your anger?

2. How does anger show that men are made in the image of God?

3. When Jesus was angry with the Pharisees he felt compassion. Do you feel compassion when you're angry? Why? Why not?

4. How did Jesus express his anger in a controlled way when he cleansed the Temple?

5. How can you follow his example?

PART TWO

STORIES OF ANGER

Identity

Respect • Control

Pride • Forgiveness • Blessing

Responding

CHAPTER 3

THE MAN WITH
A HOLE IN HIS FACE
Identity

THE FIRST THING I noticed about Roger was his smile. It was a happy, wide grin that lit up the rest of his face. And yet his smile hung crooked and gave him a goofy look. Not goofy as in dumb, but goofy as in funny—like he had a sense of humor. I looked at him and smiled in return. Not as a courtesy, but because I think anybody who saw him smile would feel like a secret, unspoken joke had been told, heard, and laughed at. And so I smiled as he and his wife entered my office.

Roger's dark brown hair hung over his forehead, giving him the appearance of a man ten years younger than his forty years. And he had a scar on his left cheek. It was shaped like a dime-sized star. He had gotten it in an unusual—no, *unusual* is the wrong word—he had gotten it in a bizarre and violent way, as I would soon find out.

His wife, Lucy, looked a bit like Nicole Kidman with her blondish red hair, sky blue eyes, and creamy white complexion. Roger was over six feet tall, and Lucy was maybe five foot two. Her eyes were steel hard, and I knew right away that Roger's smile hid something that had hurt Lucy.

They sat on the two brown leather chairs in my office, just to the side of the fireplace. I sat in a leather chair opposite them.

After a few minutes of small talk I asked them why they had come to see me. They looked at each another, and then Roger said, "We need help with our marriage."

"What's the biggest problem?"

"Roger's anger," Lucy said.

"Is that right, Roger?" I asked.

He nodded.

"I want you both to know that I'm not a professional counselor. I can assess your strengths and weaknesses, help you connect with God, and give you a game plan. But for the plan to work, you've got to put it into practice. Are you willing to do that?"

They looked at each other and nodded.

THE GROUND RULES

As a pastor and spiritual life coach, I find it helpful to explain immediately the ground rules for our meetings. I let Roger and Lucy know that I'm results oriented, so if an individual or couple I'm working with consistently fails to practice our plan of action, I'll refer them to a therapist. Such a counselor would be able and willing to spend the time needed to help them understand the root of their problem so they could overcome it. I told them that I think most of the problems we have with anger and other compulsive behaviors can be understood and managed quickly if we're willing to do some hard work.

Of course, it may take a lifetime to understand
how we got so messed up and to more fully
comprehend our identity in Christ. But
getting a handle on the problem can happen
quickly with good counsel and hard work.

"We'll work," Roger said. Lucy nodded her agreement.

Roger then touched the scar on his left cheek.

"How did that happen?" I asked.

He rubbed the scar and smiled that goofy smile. "I got mad one night, placed the barrel of a loaded pistol in my mouth, and pulled the trigger. I meant to blow my brains out, but I missed and shot a hole in my face."

I hadn't seen that coming but managed to swallow my shock without choking. "How long ago did you do that?"

"Ten years," he said. "That's when I decided to quit drinking."

"But he's still got a problem controlling his anger," Lucy said. "While he's never hurt me, when he goes into a rage he yells and threatens me. Sometimes he threatens to hurt himself."

"When I trusted Christ last year, I hoped that would put an end to my anger," Roger said.

"You mean like a magic pill?" I asked.

"Or a magic wand," Roger said.

During later sessions, the three of us talked about some of the issues I'll cover in upcoming chapters . . . issues that helped Roger understand how his personal history made him susceptible to extreme and sometimes violent anger. But first I wanted to help him grasp the spiritual root of the problem and how his new identity in Christ was the key to managing and expressing his anger in a godly way.

THE RAGING BULL

In that first session, I asked Roger to describe his anger.

"When I'm mad I feel like there's a raging bull running through the streets of my mind. No, it's worse than that," Roger said. "I feel like the bull has taken over my mind. I have no choice in the matter because the bull has overpowered me. It's like I've become the bull."

Roger's words floated in the air. I didn't say anything for a few moments as I thought about how to reply. "That's a good analogy," I said. "But are you the bull? Do you think his wildness defines who you are at the core?"

"Sometimes it seems that way," he said.

Lucy sat quietly watching the flames in the fireplace.

"That may be true," I said. "But you're not the bull." I then handed Roger and Lucy a Bible and kept one for myself.

I asked them to look up 2 Peter 1:4 with me. Once we'd all found it, I said, "Notice that we're told the Father 'has given us great and precious promises. These are the promises that enable you to share his divine nature and escape the world's corruption caused by human desires.'

"Roger, God says as a believer you share in his divine nature," I said. We then spent several minutes looking at some other truths from Scripture about our identity in Christ.

- As followers of Christ, we're new creations and everything old has passed away (2 Corinthians 5:17).

- We are already qualified to share in the inheritance of the saints (Colossians 1:12, NIV).
- We who believe in Jesus are children of God (John 1:12).
- We are "a holy nation" and "aliens and strangers" whom the apostle Peter urges "to abstain from fleshly lusts which wage war against the soul" (1 Peter 2:9, 11, NASB).

YOU'RE A NEW MAN

"The amazing truth is that there are only two families on the earth: the family of man and the family of God," I told Roger and Lucy when we'd finished reviewing the Scripture passages. "And when you trusted Christ you became a member of God's family. There are two species within humanity—those who are at home here and those who are aliens. Roger, when you trusted Christ, God made you a new man, a new creation. This is not some fairy tale but a spiritual reality that defines the true you."

"But when I'm angry I don't feel like a new man," Roger said. "I feel like that raging bull."

"Maybe that's because before you met Christ, you were a raging bull. And that bull controlled your thoughts and actions. I like how the *New American Standard Bible* refers to the bull inside you as the 'flesh.' In Ephesians 2:3, Paul said that as unbelievers we 'lived in the lusts of our flesh, indulging the desires of the flesh and of the mind.'

"The word *flesh* speaks of that part of our personalities that seeks power and pleasure apart from God. Before we knew

Christ, it also defined our essential nature—that is, the essence of our inmost being. Before you knew Christ, at your very core you were driven by your flesh, the bull, in everything you thought and did. That doesn't mean you were as bad as you could have been, but you did indulge the evil desires of your mind and body in the processing and expressing of anger."

Next, we looked up Galatians 5:19-21, a passage in which Paul lists the destructive attitudes and actions that flow from our flesh. These include "immorality, impurity, sensuality, idolatry, sorcery, enmities, strife, jealousy, outbursts of anger, disputes, dissensions, factions, envying, drunkenness, carousing, and things like these" (NASB). I asked Roger and Lucy to notice that the phrase *outbursts of anger* describes a "deed" of the flesh.

> I then said, "But what's crucial is that
> while the flesh, with all its evil desires,
> still resides in you, it no longer defines
> the real you. It's just that the bull has
> run wild for so many years that you don't
> realize it has no power over you."

"Your anger gets out of control when you allow your flesh to steal your identity, which causes you to act like the man you used to be, not the new man you are in Christ. The new and good man in you will still get angry. That's okay. But it's crucial for you to learn how to get angry without allowing the bull to use your anger to steal your identity and control your actions."

As the session wrapped up, I gave Roger an assignment.

Handing him an index card and a pen, I said, "I want you to write on the card: 'I'm a new and good man in Christ.' On the other side write out 2 Corinthians 5:17, which says, 'This means that anyone who belongs to Christ has become a new person. The old life is gone; a new life has begun!'

"Every night, before going to sleep, read both sides of the card. When you climb out of bed in the morning, read them again. When you find yourself getting angry, before the bull takes over, read the card and say this to God: 'Father, I know that I'm a new and good man in Christ. The anger I feel may not be wrong, but I know that my flesh wants to use it to take over my life and define who I am. Thank you that I'm no longer defined by the bull but by you.'"

"How will this help him manage his anger?" Lucy asked.

"It will help because he sees *himself* as the bull. He's allowed the bullish anger of his flesh to drive his thinking and actions for so long that they define him. But it's a lie. He's a new and good man in Christ, and he needs to see himself that way. Anger management begins with Roger understanding his identity. I know this is a simple exercise, but it's crucial."

For the next three weeks, I met regularly with Roger and Lucy. We were all encouraged because Roger seemed to be making progress. He wasn't getting angry as often or expressing it in harmful ways. And then one evening I got a call from Lucy.

"HE'S GOT A GUN!"

I answered the phone and heard someone sobbing. But it was worse than sobbing; the woman sounded hysterical. "Roger and I got into an argument," she said. "It got bad and he stomped into the bedroom and grabbed his pistol. He's still in the bedroom, and he's threatening to shoot us both."

*Less than one percent of surveyed men said
they become physically abusive when angry.*

"Okay," I said as I tried to figure out what to say . . . what to do. It's not every day I get a call from someone whose spouse is threatening to commit murder/suicide. In fact, that was the first and only time. I knew calling the cops would be the safe thing to do—and it's what I'd recommend to anyone else in this situation. They are trained to defuse this type of situation. But at that moment I feared that if the police showed up, Roger might shoot someone or get shot himself. And I was sure he wouldn't shoot me. "I'll be right over," I said. "In the meantime, please get yourself somewhere safe."

As I hurried out the door my wife pleaded with me to call the cops. "It'll be okay," I assured her.

Fifteen minutes later I pulled into their driveway and climbed out of my car. A moment later Lucy rushed to meet me. As she stood before me, I reached out and touched her arm. She immediately began crying uncontrollably, and she seemed to get smaller. I wondered if I had poked a hole in her soul and released the flow of tears.

"Where is he?" I asked.

"In the bedroom," she answered. "I'll show you."

"No, just tell me the way," I said.

"Go down the hall. He's in the second room to the left."

My heart pounded like a frightened rabbit's as I approached the door and slowly swung it open. After calling out, "Roger, it's me, Bill," I cautiously pushed the door open a bit more. Using the wall as a shield, I stuck my head into the room where I saw Roger sitting on the bed twirling the pistol around his right index finger like a gunslinger.

"THE BULLETS WILL GO THROUGH SHEETROCK"

"Why are you standing behind the wall?" Roger asked. "If I wanted to shoot you, the bullets would go through the sheetrock like paper."

"Oh," I said. And then I laughed as a thought occurred to me. "Roger, with your history of missing what you shoot at, I'm probably standing in a safe place."

He laughed and invited me into the room.

"Have a seat," he said, shaking his head and smiling. "I can't believe you got me to laugh, but you did."

I sat beside him on the bed and stared at the pistol, which he continued to twirl.

"Roger, could I have the gun?"

He spun the gun one more time and then slapped it into his left hand. "Good idea," he said as he emptied the bullets from the firearm and handed it to me. "I had no intention of shooting anyone. It was just a prop."

"Do you have any other firearms?" I asked.

"Yes."

"Would you mind if I kept them for a while? I think it would make Lucy feel safer. And I'd sleep better knowing you let me have them."

"Sure, you can have them," he said.

As Roger and I walked out of the bedroom, I asked, "What happened?"

"I was doing really well until Lucy got on my case about mowing the yard. She just wouldn't let up," he said. "It's not like I'm a kid and need her to manage my life. I mean, give me a break! Anyway, the bull took over and I lost it."

We talked for a few minutes and then joined Lucy in the den. Amazingly, she had calmed down and apologized to Roger for disrespecting him.

"It won't happen again," he promised. "Bill is going to keep my firearms at his house."

Hoping to turn this horrible situation around, I said, "Sometimes Christians are surprised when they discover they are just as capable of evil as they were before they knew Christ. But what happened today proves that your flesh, the angry bull, is waiting in his stall, eager to take over your life."

UNDERSTANDING YOUR NEW AND TRUE IDENTITY

I asked Lucy for a Bible. Together we looked at Romans 6:2, where Paul asks, "How shall we who died to sin still live in it?" (NASB). It's important to note, I pointed out, that Paul didn't say that our sin, or bullish anger, died. He said *we* died.

"Since none of us have died physically," I said, "Paul had to be referring to another kind of death—a spiritual death. This is deep stuff. Paul is telling us that as believers we've been spiritually identified with Christ in his death, burial, and resurrection."

"How did that happen?" Roger asked.

"I don't know," I said. "But somehow God pulled us through

time and space and placed us into Jesus during his crucifixion and resurrection. Everything that's true of him is true of us.

"Roger, consider for a moment the implications of this truth. Does the angry bull have power over Christ?"

"Of course not," he said.

"Since that's the case," I said, "it has no power over you. Paul wants you to realize it's inconsistent for you to allow your raging anger to control your life since you've died and been raised with Christ. You're a new man, identified with him. The risen Lord of the universe actually lives in you!"

ANOTHER ROSWELL INCIDENT

"Okay, now let me give you another illustration.[1] The backyard of the home I grew up in had a number of crab apple trees. One day I pulled an apple from one of the trees and popped it into my mouth. Almost immediately I regretted having done that. I expected something sweet but tasted only bitterness.

"That bitter fruit is an excellent picture of our essential nature *before* we trusted Christ. The apostle Paul described it this way: 'Among them we too all formerly lived in the lusts of our flesh, indulging the desires of the flesh and of the mind, and were by nature children of wrath, even as the rest.'[2]

"Just as that tree produced sour apples that would be left to rot, so our evil flesh produced sinful deeds that resulted in misery and death. You see this every time your anger gets out of control and runs your life."

"No kidding," Roger said.

"But suppose my dad was tired of getting only sour fruit from those trees, so he came up with a way to change the fruit.

He made a diagonal cut across the trunk of one of the trees. Then he took a fresh green section of stem, cut into a matching diagonal slice from a different tree, and spliced it on to what was left of the trunk. Next he wrapped and sealed the splice and supported the new stem with a brace. Finally he attached a tag to one of the new branches that said 'golden delicious apple.'

"Buds would begin to appear above the splice line in the months that followed. Before long, these would blossom, and then apples—golden delicious apples—would appear.

"So, Roger, if someone asked my dad what kind of tree it was, what would he have said?"

"I guess it wouldn't be a crab apple tree anymore, would it?" he asked.

"That's right. Nor would it be a crab apple/golden delicious tree."

"I think I see where you're going," Roger said. "It would be a golden delicious apple tree."

"Exactly. That would be the tree's new—and *true*—identity. But the tree would still have some identity issues. Why? Because below the graft, sucker shoots would still appear. And if they weren't cut off, they would produce crab apples. Those sucker shoots and their fruit would be usurpers deserving one thing: removal.

"In fact, my dad would have to be diligent about removing any buds below the graft. Otherwise, they would so overrun the tree that its true identity would scarcely be seen, surrounded by the wild growth from below the graft. But even if that happened, my dad wouldn't have changed the tag."

"Okay," Roger said. "I get it. He wouldn't have changed

the tag because the essential nature of the tree would remain a golden delicious apple tree."

"Exactly," I said. "The sucker shoots would have to go because they no longer represent the true identity of the tree."[3]

"The moment you trusted Christ, your old self was cut off, crucified. What you had been by nature, a child of wrath, you are no more. At this moment you're a new man."

"Paul said this another way in Galatians 2:20: 'My old self has been crucified with Christ. It is no longer I who live, but Christ lives in me. So I live in this earthly body by trusting in the Son of God, who loved me and gave himself for me.'

"But as you know, the root and base of the old trunk still remain in you. They have not changed at all. In fact, they continue trying to grow sucker shoots. But no matter how many crab apples—or sins of anger—appear in your life, by nature you're a new man.

"Roger, you've been released from the power of your raging anger," I continued. "But the first step in grasping your new identity involves knowledge. You're a new man because you've been joined with Christ, and your old man with its uncontrolled anger has no more power over you than it has over Jesus Christ. He is the golden delicious apple tree that's been grafted into you, changing your identity."

"So what happened to me this afternoon," Roger said, "is that my flesh, the sucker shoots, convinced me that their power wasn't broken. I *felt* like a crab apple tree and acted like one."

"Precisely," I said. "But regardless of how you feel in the future, you need to know that Christ has shattered the power of the old man with its destructive anger. You no longer have to give in to your anger. The sucker shoots from the base of the tree do not need to grow in your life and define your identity. You will feel them below the graft line, ready to grow and take over. When that happens, you'll need to cut them off by focusing on your true identity. In that way your life will produce thoughts and actions consistent with who you are in Christ. You'll process and express your anger as he did."

Roger looked at me with his goofy smile. "For the record, Bill, I like the bull illustration better. I suppose some guys get sour when they're angry. Personally, I feel like a wild bull has taken over. Either way, I see what you're saying: when my anger runs wild, I'm not acting from my new and true self."

"And when you let the bull run wild like you did today, you're endangering Lucy," I said.

Roger nodded his head in agreement. "I know," he said.

Concerned for Lucy, I looked at her and said, "I know you're committed to seeing your marriage work, but abusive behavior of any kind from Roger is unacceptable. Do you understand that?"

"Yes, I understand."

"In the future, if anything like this even starts to take place, you need to remove yourself at once. Okay?"

"Okay," she said.

"And Roger, while nobody got hurt today, at least not physically, your actions terrified Lucy. You've got to draw a line and never cross it again. You can't allow yourself to verbally or physically threaten her. Will you commit to continue meeting with me or another accountability partner to help you keep your anger in check?"

"Absolutely," he said.

Shortly after this conversation, I headed home. In that moment I knew that Roger got it, like a kid who's figured out a complicated math problem. It was hard to believe that a few hours earlier he had been raging.

WHY I TOLD YOU ABOUT ROGER

I've told you Roger's story because I've never met a man whose life changed more radically after he grasped the idea of his new identity in Christ. The more Roger meditated on Bible verses that described the new him, the more he was able to cut off the sucker shoots of anger that threatened to steal his identity. He also started learning how to rely on the power of Christ within him to direct his thoughts and actions.

I believe you too can know the kind of change Roger experienced. If we were meeting in my office I'd give you an important assignment. First, I'd ask you to write the "Truths to Live By" on the next page on an index card and review them daily. Second, I'd ask you to write the verses that follow on cards and meditate on them throughout each day until you've got them memorized. And then I'd recommend that you review them daily. As you meditate on the verses ask God to enable you to see yourself as a new and true man in Christ.

Of course, as I noted earlier, while knowing our identity is at the core of anger management, there are other crucial issues we must understand. And in the next chapter we'll look at a key source of anger for most men.

TRUTHS TO LIVE BY

- By God's grace and with hard work, I can understand and manage my anger.
- I'm a new man, a good man, a son of God, an alien, and part of a holy nation. This is my true identity in Christ.
- When I lose control of my anger, I've allowed my flesh to steal my identity and define who I am.
- While I lived for years under the domination of my flesh and the angry bull within me, its power over me has been broken through Christ.
- When I find myself getting angry, I'll say this prayer: "Father, I know that I'm a new and good man in Christ. The anger I feel may not be wrong, but I know that my flesh wants to use it to take over my life and define who I am. Thank you that I'm no longer defined by the bull but by you."

STRENGTHEN THE GOOD MAN

And because of his glory and excellence, he has given us great and precious promises. These are the promises that enable you to share his divine nature and escape the world's corruption caused by human desires. (2 PETER 1:4)

May you be filled with joy, always thanking the Father. He has enabled you to share in the inheritance that belongs to his people, who live in the light. (COLOSSIANS 1:11-12)

But to all who believed him and accepted him, he gave the right to become children of God. (JOHN 1:12)

But you are a chosen people, a royal priesthood, a holy nation, a people belonging to God, that you may declare the praises of him who called you out of darkness into his wonderful light.

Once you were not a people, but now you are the people of God; once you had not received mercy, but now you have received mercy. Dear friends, I urge you, as aliens and strangers in the world, to abstain from sinful desires, which war against your soul. (1 PETER 2:9-11, NIV)

DISCUSSION QUESTIONS

1. When you're angry, do you feel more like a raging bull or a sour apple? Why?

2. How has allowing your flesh to drive your anger affected how you see yourself?

3. How does the Bible describe your true identity as a follower of Christ? In addition to the verses above, you may want to look up 2 Corinthians 5:17.

4. How does the crab apple tree illustrate how your new and true nature relates to the flesh, or bull, within you?

5. How will knowing your true identity help you better manage and control your anger? Be as specific as you can.

CHAPTER 4

THE MAN WHO WITHHELD SEX FROM HIS WIFE
Respect

I'VE BEEN TO only two professional fights in my life. And I wouldn't have gone to either if one of the fighters hadn't brought me along to watch.

I had no idea sitting ringside would be such a rush. Of course, knowing one of the fighters added to the excitement. The fighter's name was Austin. He grew up in Austin, Texas. Good thing he didn't grow up in Waxahachie—a small town in Texas. That was his joke, not mine.

The bell rang for round one. I knew what to expect from Austin because he had told me he wasn't the aggressor in a fight. "I back up. I let the other guy come after me."

"Why?"

"Because I'm a counterpuncher. When you see me backing up, don't worry about it. Every aggressor makes a mistake, and when they do—*bam*! I hammer them."

I'm glad he told me that because Austin's opponent came after him fast and hard. The guy was shorter and built like a smaller version of Mike Tyson. For two minutes Austin backed up and dodged one punch after another. And then it was over.

Austin ducked a crossing right and followed with a powerful right uppercut. *Bam!* His opponent's eyes rolled into the top of his head, and he fell back hard. His head hit the canvas and bounced once. Austin raised his hands in victory and smiled triumphantly.

A week later I met with Austin and Holly, his wife, in my office. Austin was an impressive man. Only twenty-eight, he already owned a thriving construction company that built high-end homes. At 5 foot 11 inches, he weighed in at 175 pounds and wore his black hair marine short. His wife was equally impressive. A tall, attractive woman, she had short blond hair, angel green eyes, and a cheerful look. She worked as a buyer for a chain of clothing stores.

DISRESPECT TRIGGERS ANGER

They entered my office without speaking a word or even looking at each other and sat in the two leather chairs. Holly sat upright with her arms crossed and her jaw locked. Austin appeared relaxed with a smirk on his face. He seemed to be enjoying her misery.

I broke the tense silence. "What's going on?"

"Holly is upset because we don't have sex as often as she wants to."

"Oh, really, Austin? You think that maybe I'm too sexually demanding since I want to make love with you more than once a month." Holly spoke with a hard edge that I didn't expect.

"I've been busy. You know that."

"You've always been busy. But until three months ago you

always found time for sex three or four times a week. I know you're mad at me for something. I just don't know what."

Austin smiled. "Why would I be mad at you?"

In that moment I knew Holly was right. It was Austin's smile that gave him away. I had seen it a week earlier at the fight when he won. Withholding sex would mimic his boxing style. Instead of attacking Holly, he backed off. No aggressive verbal attack on his part. I needed to discover what triggered his anger.

"Holly, would you mind if I spent a few minutes alone with Austin?"

She tilted her head, looking at Austin and then at me. "Sure. Go ahead." She picked up her purse and walked out the door, closing it behind her.

"What did she do to make you mad?"

"What makes you think I'm mad?"

"Austin, let's not play games here, okay? Just shoot straight with me."

"I'm just giving her a taste of her own medicine."

"How's that?"

"I got tired of her saying she was too tired for sex or wasn't in the mood."

"Do you think she said that to get even with you?"

"No."

"She said until three months ago you had been having sex three or four times a week. Is that true?"

"Yeah, it's true."

"So how many times did she *not* want to make love?"

"Okay, it wasn't that often. But it made me mad."

"Why?"

"I don't know. I guess I felt she disrespected me and my needs."

"So you got mad, and instead of talking it through you decided to disrespect her need for intimacy?

"That pretty much sums it up."

"Austin, let's assume for a minute that she disregarded your needs. On a scale of one to ten, how bad would that act be compared to what you've been doing for the last three months? Remember, she acted unintentionally. You meant to hurt her."

"I know. I get your point."

"I'm curious, Austin. How could you live with a woman so beautiful and not make love to her? I remember when I first got married I decided to withhold sex from Cindy. I figured that would straighten her out. I made it maybe two days."

"I guess I'm better at staying mad when I feel disrespected," he said.

25 percent of surveyed men get angry when their wives aren't in the mood for sex.

19 percent usually express anger by withdrawing affection and communication.

40 percent occasionally express anger that way.

Austin's comment got my attention. It seemed that disrespect had triggered a prolonged anger that he refused to release. I hoped he could discover why. I knew from previous conversations with Austin that his wife wasn't the only person he torpedoed when he felt disrespected.

Holly rejoined us, and Austin told her why he had been withholding sex.

Holly sat silently, but her stillness seemed sharp enough to stab Austin. She finally spoke in a controlled voice. "You figure out how to deal with your anger . . . or else." The words didn't sound as harsh to the ear as they appear to the eye when read. She spoke sweetly, and her words lingered in the room like a fragrance.

But Austin didn't hear her tone. "Or else what?" he said, challenging her.

"Or else," she hesitated. Tears trickled down her cheeks. "We'll be living in torment. And I . . . we . . . don't want that."

As we talked more about how Austin's rejection of his wife's advances was hurting their marriage, he slowly realized how misguided his anger had been.

I took some time at the end of the session to talk with them about a man's need for respect. "I think it ties in to our being created in the image of God. Just as God desires the respect of man, and will ultimately get it from everyone, so men desire respect. In the Garden of Eden God gave mankind dominion over the earth. But before the creation of Eve, it was Adam who named the animals.[1] By doing so he proved himself their master. In other words, from the beginning man exercised a role of leadership over the earth and wildlife."

"Even now after the Fall, men are still wired to understand and subdue the earth. And with that genetic drive comes an equally strong need for respect from the world around them—the world they hope to subdue."

"In the context of marriage, God commands men to love their wives and women to *respect* their husbands.[2] Paul's command underscores the significance of a man's need for respect."

30 percent of surveyed men said disrespect is the main cause of anger for them.

"So what you're saying is that Austin's need for respect was put there by God?" Holly said.

"That's right. The problem is that this God-given need can easily be channeled destructively. When that happens, any act of disrespect, or perceived disrespect, can trigger inappropriate anger."

"Like when I got mad at Holly for refusing my advances?"

"Exactly."

NOBODY ELSE IS YOUR PARENT

"Okay. So how do I keep from overreacting?" Austin asked.

"Between now and next week, whenever you find yourself getting mad ask yourself, 'Am I really being disrespected? Or is it a perceived act of disrespect?' At the end of each day, talk with Holly about what you experienced. Next week share what you've learned with me."

When we met the next week Austin was stunned by how many times he had gotten angry about *perceived* acts of disrespect. As he talked about getting mad, he repeatedly referred to demanding customers and subcontractors as "leeches."

I pointed this out to him and asked why he felt they were leeches.

At first he had no idea why he would call them that. And then he surprised himself with an answer. "I think maybe it's got to do with my mother."

"Go on," I said.

"She was an alcoholic . . . an emotional black hole. Instead of nurturing her kids, she wanted us to nurture her. When I was sixteen, she was in a horrible car wreck and was hospitalized for three months. She almost lost her left arm. When she came home in a wheelchair, she asked me to give her shoulder and back massages. She said I had healing hands. I did it a time or two, but it drained me too much—like a leech sucking out my blood. If she refused to respect me and my needs, how could she expect me to respect and meet hers? And so I stopped. I just didn't have the emotional strength to care for her like that. I resented her. I also remember turning off my compassion like the light of a lamp."

"No wonder you're angry," I said. "And no wonder you lack compassion for people who seem demanding or disrespectful. But, Austin, nobody else is your mother. And nobody will ever do to you what she did."

Austin sat silently for a couple of minutes with his face in his hands. Holly leaned over and put her hand on his shoulder.

THE RESPECT BANK

When he finally looked up he said, "I hear what you're saying, but why would my mom's neediness still be causing me problems?"

I leaned to my right, picked up a picture from the floor, and handed it to Austin. "I planned on showing you something today, and now seems like a good time," I said.

THE RESPECT BANK

After glancing at the picture, he said, "A piggy bank will help put things in perspective?"

"I hope so," I said. "Every man has what I call a 'respect bank' in his heart. If his parents, coaches, teachers, family, and friends give him a lot of respect and affirmation as he's growing up, he may get through childhood and adolescence with a respect surplus."

I then handed him a second picture, which showed a piggy bank stuffed to overflowing with coins.

THE SURPLUS RESPECT BANK

"When a young man enters adulthood with a respect surplus and someone shows him disrespect, it has little effect on him. His sense of self-worth isn't threatened, so it's easier for him to manage the little anger he may experience.

"Unfortunately, many men grow up with a respect deficit.

Their parents and other important people in their lives gave them little respect and affirmation. That's what happened with you and your mother and even your father. I remember when we were driving home from your fight and I asked you about your dad. You said he attended your athletic events, but you never quite measured up to his high standard of competition. I got the impression that while you respect him, you don't think he respects you. I'm not knocking your parents; I'm just saying that their lack of affirmation and encouragement created a deficit in your respect bank."

THE DEFICIT RESPECT BANK

Austin interrupted. "And since my bank is empty, when Holly or people at work disrespect me—or seem to—I overreact and get angry. And my anger is an attempt to force them to make a deposit in my respect bank."[3]

"You've nailed it," I said. "But there's one more important element to consider. When you get angry at people who disrespect you and later refer to them as leeches, it may be that you feel toward them like you did toward your parents. And so you react against them in an effort to replace not only the respect you feel those people took from you, but the respect your parents took. You're not just reacting with anger for their offense, but for the disrespect you felt for years from your mom and dad. Not only can no one else do what they did to you, but no one else should be punished for what they did."

"So you're saying that I've been trying to force Holly, along with many other people, to make up for all the respect my parents failed to give me?"

"It seems that way to me. And it might also explain why you were able to withhold sex from Holly for so long. Since you came into marriage with a deficit in your respect bank, even her best efforts couldn't give you enough respect to create a surplus. To make matters worse, your anger had the opposite effect of what you intended. Instead of treating you with more respect, she got mad and treated you with less."

"What can he do to create a surplus in his respect bank?" Holly asked.

"Before addressing that question, let me ask you one," I said. "Do either of you think it would be possible to get so much respect and affirmation that you could say, 'That's enough; I never want any more'?"

They both laughed and assured me they couldn't.

"Let me give you an illustration from my marriage," I said. "I make an effort every day to tell my wife, Cindy, how beautiful I think she is. Whenever we see a stunning sunset, painting, or anything else that grabs our attention, I'll say, 'It's beautiful, isn't it?' She'll always agree. And then I'll say, 'But it's not as beautiful as you, and I get to see you every day.'

"One evening I asked her, 'Cindy, do you ever get tired of me telling you how beautiful I think you are? Should I cut down on the affirmation?' 'Oh, no!' she said. 'I never get enough!'"

We laughed together, and then I said, "Men are the same

way when it comes to respect. . . . We can never get enough. The fact is that our parents, wives, children, bosses, and friends are incapable of filling our respect bank. Only God can do that."

Then I asked him, "How do you win the respect of an opponent in the ring?"

"With my smartness, skill, stamina, speed, and toughness."

"And how do you develop those?"

"The only way I know is through disciplined training."

"When you train, do you try to anticipate how you'll respond to an opponent?"

"Sure. That's why I spar. It perfects my skills and makes me tough. It helps me think better when I'm in a real fight."

"You mentioned thinking. Do you ever get mad when an opponent trash-talks you or connects with a powerful punch?"

"I train not to get mad. If I get mad, then all of my experience goes out the window because I throw wild punches."

"Suppose for a moment that every day you're involved in a spiritual battle . . . because you are. And suppose that every word and act of disrespect or perceived disrespect is a jab thrown by an opponent."

"In order to respond with skill, stamina, speed, and toughness, you need a training routine. A routine that will help you keep your cool when someone trash-talks you or hits you with a disrespectful act. Such a routine involves strengthening the way you see yourself. And that demands depositing into your respect bank the kind of truth that will create a surplus."

While I waited for Austin to respond, I grabbed a Bible from the round table between us.

After several moments he said, "No wonder my anger is out of control. I never even knew I was in a fight, and so I did nothing to prepare."

"The training routine is simple, Austin. But it demands discipline. It's based on the biblical truth that you're a new man in Christ." I flipped my Bible open to the book of John. "Your true and new identity is wrapped up in Jesus. And it's based on the fact that you are of infinite value to God. It's one thing for me to tell you that and another thing for you to believe it's true at the core of your being. Yet how do we determine the value of anything? By the price paid for it. And the price God paid for you was the life of his Son. John 3:16 tells us, 'For God loved the world so much that he gave his one and only Son, so that everyone who believes in him will not perish but have eternal life.'"

"I realize this verse has been read and recited so many times that it often loses its punch. But if you substitute your name for the word *world*, you realize that Jesus is telling you God loved *you* enough to send his Son to die so you could have a friendship with him. God would not have allowed his Son to suffer for you unless he valued and respected you.

"Austin, would you doubt the love of someone who died for you?"

"Never," he said.

"Of course not," I said. "And there's another passage that contains a complementary truth. Later, on the night before his death, Jesus prayed for his present and future disciples. During that prayer he said in John 17:23, 'May they experience such perfect unity that the world will know that you sent me and that you love them as much as you love me.'"

I handed the Bible to Austin again and asked him to read that verse aloud for Holly and me. After he read it, I asked him if he saw something mind-blowing in it.

"Jesus said that God the Father loves me as much as he loves Jesus," Austin said. "I've never seen that before."

"There are no favorites in God's family," I said. "Austin, Jesus prayed this knowing the disciples would abandon him and Peter would deny him. Yet Jesus said his Father loved these weak men as much as he loved his perfect Son."

We talked briefly about this concept, and then I gave Austin a training routine. "There are several things you need to do," I said.

"First, you must memorize and then review John 3:16 and John 17:23 every day. Each time you review the verses, take a moment and thank God that he loves and respects you. Thank him that the true and new you is a man of infinite worth to him.

"Second, when you feel disrespected throughout the day, consider yourself in a sparring match. Think of it as a situation God put you in to strengthen your character—the true and new you. Quickly tell God, 'Thanks for filling my respect bank. Enable me to act as a man of infinite worth even when I feel otherwise.'

"Third, continue to determine whether the words and actions that anger you are real or perceived acts of disrespect. In either case, refuse to act on your anger. Control your response just as you would if you were in the boxing ring.

"Fourth, keep a daily list of how you're doing in each of these three other disciplines and report to me next week."

THE SECOND FIGHT

The second professional fight I ever attended surprised me more than the first. I think it's because I expected my friend to let his opponent be the aggressor. Instead, Austin took the fight to him. As the fight progressed I thought Austin would win because of his superior skills and much higher punch count. But in the fourth round a powerful jab opened a cut over his right eye, and the ringside doctor called the fight.

Afterward I asked him why he changed tactics. "I don't know," he said, as he rubbed the mouse over his eye. "I think it's got something to do with how I view myself. But maybe not."

"What do you mean?" I asked.

"I'm not as angry. And an angry me always backed up and counterpunched. I think taking on my feelings of disrespect so aggressively enabled me to stop letting my anger knock me around and dictate the pace of my life. I suspect that carried over to the ring. I'm just more comfortable being the aggressor than before."

TRUTHS TO LIVE BY
- God wired me to need respect, and that's a good thing.
- My need for respect can become distorted so that any real or perceived act of disrespect can trigger inappropriate anger.
- Nobody else can do to me what my parents did to me, and nobody else should be punished for what they did.
- If I've got a deficit in my respect bank, then I may try to

use anger to force others to treat me respectfully in order to fill my bank.

- My anger usually fosters disrespect in those around me.
- Only God can fill my respect bank.
- My respect bank is filled as I embrace my true and new identity in Christ.
- When I feel disrespected, I won't act on my initial impulse and throw wild verbal or physical punches.
- Allowing God to fill my respect bank requires that I put into practice a spiritual training routine.

STRENGTHEN THE GOOD MAN

For God loved the world so much that he gave his one and only Son, so that everyone who believes in him will not perish but have eternal life. (JOHN 3:16)

May they experience such perfect unity that the world will know that you sent me and that you love them as much as you love me. (JOHN 17:23)

DISCUSSION QUESTIONS

1. How do you feel when someone disrespects you?

2. Did your dad give you his blessing when you were growing up? That is, did he offer you words of affirmation and encouragement that indicated he believed in you? God the Father did this for Jesus at the Lord's baptism when he said, "This is my dearly loved Son, who brings me great joy" (Matthew 3:17). Explain why you think your dad did or didn't give you his blessing.

3. Did your mother give you her blessing when you were growing up? Explain.

4. Do you feel respected at home? At work? Explain.

5. How full is your respect bank, using a scale of one to ten, with one being empty and ten being full?

6. How do you try to fill your respect bank?

7. How can God fill your respect bank?

8. How will you put into practice this chapter's training routine?

CHAPTER 5

THE MAN WHO YELLED
AT HIS DAUGHTER
Control

BECAUSE BRIAN HAD asked if he could bring his "out of control" daughter to meet with me, I expected a teenage girl with spiked hair, tattoos, a nose ring, a flashing tongue ring, five or six eyebrow rings, and an attitude that said, *Don't mess with me!* If she didn't sport heavy metal on her face and in her mouth, I figured she'd at least be mouthy.

Instead I saw a girl with bright brown eyes, short shaggy hair, and a demure smile. She was wearing jeans that looked like they came from Goodwill and a black blouse that might have come from Old Navy. I could imagine her walking down the runway as an edgy teen model at a fashion show promoting purity . . . she looked as cool and wholesome as a glass of skim milk. I figured her for a thespian hooked on Shakespeare.

Her father, Brian, introduced us, and Thea surprised me with extended eye contact and a firm handshake. *This isn't what I expected*, I thought.

Brian had told me he and his wife had tried *everything* to help Thea get her act together. They had met with the school counselor. They had seen a psychologist. They had taken away privileges. Nothing had worked. He jokingly said they even considered wrapping her legs and arms with duct tape and putting a strip across her mouth, but they figured she'd somehow squirm out. I didn't laugh.

Brian said the psychologist had administered a battery of tests and concluded, unlike the school counselor, that Thea did *not* have ADHD—attention deficit hyperactivity disorder. He said that news gave him a rush of relief. But panic replaced relief when the psychologist went on to say that Thea was a slow learner who struggled with math and foreign languages, which explained her poor grades in algebra and Spanish. The fact that she scored off the charts in creativity did nothing to appease Brian's panic.

"HELP ME FIX THEA"

In fact, the psychologist's expert opinion annoyed Brian. He attributed Thea's problems with algebra and Spanish not to a learning disability, but to her refusal to work. But he feared she had bigger issues than laziness. A month before he had found a marijuana roach in the car ashtray. Thea swore one of the kids she carpooled to school with must have left it there as a joke. And then a few days before he had checked out her MySpace page and was stunned by the racy picture she had posted there.

All of this prompted Brian to ask if I'd help him "fix Thea."

I'd dealt with enough parents to suspect Brian had an issue of his own. And it didn't take me long to figure it out.

After introducing Thea, Brian left with a promise to return in *exactly* one hour.

After we were seated I asked her, "What seems to be the matter?"

She patted the life-size porcelain Dalmatian that sat attentively beside her chair. "I wish I knew," she said with a sigh.

Something about her manner, the way she spoke and gently patted the dog, made me like her.

"What has Dad told you?" she asked.

"He said you're out of control. He said you're undisciplined."

"It's true. I have a hard time focusing. But is that all he told you?"

"What else is there?"

"You mean what else beside the fact that he erupted when he found a joint in my car and freaked out when he saw the picture I had posted on MySpace?"

Normally, I would view such a statement as a diversion . . . an attempt to direct the conversation onto someone else.

But the emotion with which Thea spoke told me I needed to probe for more information.

"What did you mean when you said he erupted and freaked out?"

"I mean he yelled at me. He called me a stupid, lazy tramp. He said if I didn't get my act together, I'd end up on the street living under a bridge."

"Does he yell at your mother and brother?"

"Of course he yells at them—but only once in a while. He seems to yell at me all the time."

"Has he always done that?"

Thea bit her bottom lip for a moment as she thought. "Yes, I think he has."

"I'm sorry to hear that, Thea. Would you mind if I talk with your dad about how he expresses his anger toward you?"

During the remainder of our meeting I learned that Thea possessed an exceptional interest in writing and photography. Equally important, I learned she was excessively impulsive. Though I'm not a psychologist, I had recently been consulting with a physician who specialized in treating impulse control disorder (ISD). I suspected this condition, not ADHD or a learning disability, might explain her lack of discipline and follow-through as well as many of her foolish decisions. I had an unusual question to ask her before I could be sure her problem stemmed from impulsivity. But this first meeting wasn't the right time to ask it.

More pressing was my need to talk with Brian about why he repeatedly abused his daughter with angry outbursts. After talking with Thea, I thought I had a better understanding of why he reacted to her this way; my next challenge would be to help him make the same discovery.

DOES YELLING REALLY HELP?

A week later I met with Brian. He looked tired as he sat in the brown chair by the fireplace. "Thea and I got in an argument last night."

"What happened?"

Brian ran his hands through his hair and said, "Bill, with Thea it's one thing after another. She won't clean her bedroom and bathroom. She's barely passing algebra and Spanish. She posted that trashy picture on MySpace. And last night I overheard her mentioning something about cocaine and a party to a friend. When she got off the phone I accused her of using drugs. Thea insisted she wasn't. She said her friend saw a guy snorting coke at a frat party when she was visiting her brother at college. And then she told me I shouldn't be eavesdropping on her conversations.

"After that she stomped into her room, slamming and locking the door. I demanded she open the door. When she refused, I kicked it open and stormed into her room. I could see she was scared, but she didn't back down. Instead she yelled at me, 'Nice job with the door. Are you going to hit me next?' And then she said I was out of control.

"I didn't touch her, but I felt like shaking some sense into her. Instead I yelled, hoping my words would get through. I told her I know how to clean up after myself and finish any job I start. I said that I don't make phony excuses when I fail. And then I told her she was a lazy idiot who made one bad decision after another, never kept her promises, and was totally disrespectful. I could tell those last words got through. She started crying and told me to get out of her room. And so I left. We haven't spoken since." Brian stared at me for several moments, silent. And then he said, "I really blew it, didn't I?"

*32 percent of surveyed men said
they occasionally express their
anger with verbal abuse.*

I nodded my head. "Those were harsh words, Brian. I'm curious; do you think they worked?"

That question stunned Brian. "What do you mean?"

"Did yelling and insulting Thea straighten her out? Did it prompt her to clean her room, study harder, put up a new picture on MySpace, and pick new friends?"

"No. Nothing I've done has worked. What are you getting at?"

"Brian, do you verbally abuse other people who frustrate you?"

"I'll occasionally get mad at my wife or son. And I've been known to yell at people at work. But nobody gets under my skin like Thea."

"Why is that?"

"She just won't get her act together no matter how much support or direction I give her."

"Do you feel she disrespects you?"

"Definitely."

THE ILLUSION OF CONTROL

"Do you think maybe your anger is an attempt to force her to conform to your wishes?"

"No doubt about that. If she'd do what I tell her, I wouldn't need to yell."

"Have you ever considered the possibility that she, and others, don't have to bow to your wishes?"

"But she's my daughter."

"That's true, but she's sixteen years old. The parenting techniques that worked a few years ago aren't effective now. You need to begin treating her more like an adult. Besides, she's very different from you. She's creative, artistic, and impulsive. You're goal oriented, organized, and driven."

"I'm artistic too," he said. "That's how I built my ad agency."

"So you have that in common?"

"Yes, and she's the life of a party, just like me."

"You must see a lot of potential in her."

"I do. That's what makes her lack of direction and drive so hard for me. I see myself in her and want her to achieve her potential."

"But she's not you," I said. "And you'll never make her conform to your expectations no matter how mad you get or how much you yell."

"I can't help myself," he said. "When I tell her what to do and she says she'll do it but doesn't follow through, I get mad."

"How does she respond to your anger?"

"She shuts down and refuses to talk. Or she goes into her room and closes the door. That infuriates me."

"Brian, you can't control another person and force her into the mold of your demands and expectations. But you can control your anger. And if you hope to cultivate a healthy relationship with Thea and provide her the support she needs, you must do so.

"You brought Thea here so I could help you fix *her*. I think you need to focus on getting your anger under control. Thea's got some serious issues. But your angry outbursts are hurting her deeply and compounding her struggles. After what happened last night, don't you agree?"

"I've always had a hard time controlling my temper. But I don't get mad that often. It's just that Thea makes me madder than anybody else. When I get mad at her, I sometimes say mean things—things I know hurt her. Things I later regret."

I handed Brian a Bible and had him turn to Luke 15:11-32, the story of the Prodigal Son—the young man who demanded his inheritance from his father, took it, and squandered it with wild living in a distant land. In a state of despair the son came to his senses and returned to his father, who forgave him and restored him to a position of honor.

"Did that father try to control his son?" I asked.

"No."

"Would you say he respected his son's autonomy?"

"Yes."

"Brian, while his son was an adult and Thea is an adolescent, there are some key principles here that you need to consider. The father didn't yell and insult his son for preferring money over him. He didn't verbally abuse him in an effort to change his mind. He didn't follow him to the distant land. He respected his freedom. Since the father in this story represents God, it teaches us that God respects the freedom his children have to act on their own. God doesn't impose his will on us, and we must not impose our will on others.

"Consider how Jesus dealt with Peter. He knew Peter would deny him three times, but Jesus didn't try to control Peter's behavior with degrading or angry comments. Instead, Jesus assured Peter of his future usefulness to the Kingdom of God."

"It's okay to give counsel, advice, and direction, but we can't make another adult—or near adult—conform to our will. And while there are consequences and rewards for a person's choices, a person is free to make them."

"That's just not true. I *can* make Thea obey me."

"You may lock Thea in her room, but you can't prevent

her from sneaking out at night. You may make her sit at her desk, but you can't make her study. You may force her to attend church, but you can't make her love God. And when you get mad and yell at her, she may do what you demand, but *all such compliance is an illusion of control.*"

RECOGNIZE PEOPLE'S FREEDOM

"If God doesn't make *us* comply with *his* wishes," I asked Brian, "why should *we* force others to comply with *ours*? When you use anger to force Thea's conformity, do you think you may be trying to 'out-god' God? That's what the ancient Pharisees tried to do with Jesus. And it's what they did with the Jewish people. Those legalists added man-made rules to God's moral code and demanded absolute obedience. With them a person was either in or out depending on how completely he or she complied with their rules. And when Jesus refused to bow to their demands, they had him killed. Until you realize God hasn't given you the power to force Thea, or anyone else, to comply with your wishes or demands, you'll have a hard time managing your anger."

"So you're suggesting I say nothing to her about her behavior?"

"No, I'm not saying that. Jesus calls us to a high moral code—the same one he lived by. But he doesn't force us to live by that code. I'm suggesting you follow his example and respectfully make your thoughts and wishes known. As her father, you need to help Thea think through the positive and negative consequences of her choices. And you need to be sure and follow through with rewards or punishments. At the same time, you want to be sure not to protect her from any negative consequences a bad choice might bring.

"But in the midst of that, you need to respect her freedom to make her own decisions. The same is true of your wife, son, employees, and friends. When someone disappoints you by not complying with your wishes, you need to respect that decision instead of getting mad and using verbal abuse to try to control them."

"But what if Thea doesn't change? She'll destroy her life. I can't trust her with such freedom."

"Brian, you're not getting it," I said gently. "She's free to do as she chooses, whether or not you acknowledge it. Sometimes we have to trust God to work in the lives of other people. I know from my conversation with Thea that she believes in Christ. That means Christ lives in her."

"Do you think you could trust him to work in her and to change her from within? Could it be that using your anger to blast away at her resistance shows a lack of faith in God?"

Brian shifted in his chair. "I guess I never thought of it that way," he said. "In the past, whenever I tried to control my anger I did okay for a while. And then Thea, or someone else, would do something stupid and I'd get mad and yell at them."

THE ASSIGNMENT

As our meeting came to a close, I told Brian, "Getting your anger under control isn't accomplished by telling yourself you won't get mad. You've got to have a healthy and accurate view of yourself and other people. I've got a game plan for you this week that will help." I handed Brian an index card and a pen.

"Write on the card: 'People are free to make choices. I can give advice, but I can't control their decisions,'" I said. "On the other side of the card write Proverbs 19:11: 'A man's discretion makes him slow to anger, and it is his glory to overlook a transgression' (NASB).

"I want you to carry that card with you all week and read it five or six times a day. The word *discretion* in Proverbs 19:11 means 'to decide responsibly.' The new man in you is capable of deciding responsibly how to give advice and how to respect the freedom other people have to accept or reject your advice.

"The second part of your assignment involves Thea. Don't you think you owe her an apology?"

"Yes, I suppose so."

"When you apologize I want you to explain to her what you've learned about your anger and how you've used it to try and control her. Let her know you're asking God for the wisdom you need to manage your anger, so that when you're mad you'll respectfully express your thoughts in a way that acknowledges her freedom."

"Wait a minute, Bill," Brian said. "Won't she think I'm giving her permission to run wild?"

"Not if you explain that she has responsibilities. She's free to make choices that will carry consequences. That won't change. What will be different is that you'll no longer try to use anger to force her to comply with your wishes. You can be assertive and kind without insulting and demeaning her. You can be directive *and* kindhearted. Because you're a new and good man, the true you is free from the destructive power of your controlling anger. As you meditate on the truths you've written on that card, I believe God's Spirit will help you see that you can't control people with your anger. And you'll begin to allow the new and true you in Christ to manage your anger."

One week later I met with Thea again. She told me that things were much better with her dad and that he seemed to have a better handle on his anger. A single question had nagged me since our meeting the week before—the question that would reveal whether her impulsivity was at the root of much of her behavior. Her answer, I knew, could lead to another outburst of anger from her dad.

THINKING WHILE YOU'RE ANGRY

"Thea, I'd like to ask you a question. It's a tough one. Is that okay?"

She hesitated and looked down at her hands. "Sure, go ahead," she said.

"Do you shoplift?"

Thea looked up at me, then quickly glanced away.

"You don't want to, but stealing gives you a rush," I said. "Later you feel guilty."

Thea said nothing for at least a minute. Nor did I. Finally she confessed, "I steal stuff I don't even need. How did you know?"

"I didn't know for sure. But during our meeting last week I thought you might suffer from something called impulse control disorder, or ICD. Many counselors mistake ICD for

ADHD because the two have features in common. Girls who suffer from ICD often shoplift. It not only releases their anxiety, it also feels good. I suspect some of the unwise choices you make are impulsive. And I think your problems with Spanish and algebra may stem from the fact that they require intense concentration on subjects that bore you. The good news is that you can deal with this issue."

In that moment, Thea wasn't concerned about that. She had a more immediate concern. "Are you going to tell Dad about my shoplifting?"

"Do you think he needs to know?"

"He'll go ballistic."

"Eventually you'll get caught, and then he'll find out from the police. Is that what you want?"

"I'll quit."

"Have you told yourself that before?"

"Of course . . . lots of times. But why does he need to know?"

"So he can help you get through this."

"I'm afraid of what he'll do when he finds out." Finally, with tears streaming down her face, she said, "Okay, I'll tell him, if you're with me."

I called Brian in from the other room where he was waiting for Thea. He sat down in the chair beside hers.

"Daddy, I've got to tell you something. This is hard because I know you'll get mad."

Brian reached out and took Thea's right hand in his. "It's okay."

Thea choked back tears as she told Brian what she had done. I knew her confession reinforced Brian's belief that she was irresponsible. His face flushed, and before he could say anything, I asked Thea if she would step out of my office for a few minutes.

As soon as the door shut, Brian said, "This is exactly why she can't be trusted with freedom. She's not only irresponsible, she's a thief. I wonder what else she's been doing that I know nothing about. How do you think this would have reflected on me if she had been caught?"

29 percent of surveyed men always or often get angry when they see someone as incompetent, selfish, messy, or inconsiderate.

"It's okay that you're angry, Brian. She's done something foolish and illegal. She's hurt you. But what's the best way to communicate your anger right now? If you lash out at her with angry insults, do you think that will help her get past this? When Jesus got mad at the Pharisees, Scripture says he also felt sympathy for them.[1] Brian, what do you think Thea is going through right now?"

Brian stood and walked over to the window, looking out at Mt. Hood in the distance. He turned and shook his head. "I'm not used to this," he said. "When I get mad at Thea, I usually just let 'er rip."

He pulled an index card out of his shirt pocket—the one on which he had written the game plan for his anger. He read one side and then flipped it over and read the other.

"I'm not sure what she's going through. She's never been open with me."

Fortunately, that would soon change. I called Thea back in, and when she realized Brian wasn't going to blast her with angry words, she relaxed and talked openly. The more he listened, the better he understood her struggles. When our meeting ended, I hoped it was the beginning of a new chapter in their relationship.

THE TRUE SOURCE OF SELF-RESPECT

A few days later Brian and I met. After he had updated me on how he and Thea were doing, I brought up something he had mentioned during our last meeting. "You asked me how it would have reflected on you if Thea was caught stealing."

"That would have been bad news," he said.

"How so?"

"It would have made me look like an incompetent parent and a weak Christian."

"Did that thought add to your anger?"

"Sure. I don't like the idea of my daughter causing others to disrespect me."

"That makes sense. Men want to be respected, and it's reasonable that you'd get mad at someone, especially a family member, if you thought she had hurt your reputation. But if she had been caught and you had gotten angry, would your damaged name have justified treating Thea with contempt?"

"I suppose not," he said.

"Ultimately, if your sense of personal worth and self-respect flow from what others think of you, then you're in for a bumpy ride. If you live long enough, you or someone you love will do something that will reflect badly on you. That's why it's crucial for your identity to rest in who you are in Christ. The new and good you in him cannot be tarnished by what other people think of you."

Brian reflected on what I had just told him. "I understand what you're saying. But when I'm angry, I'm not thinking about my spiritual identity or what the person I'm mad at may be feeling."

"That's an honest statement," I said. "But you can train yourself to think about such things, even when you're angry. That's why Solomon said 'a man's discretion makes him slow to anger.' The new you isn't controlled by your flesh and its angry passion. The good man in you is nurtured and strengthened when you seek to obey God by thinking through your anger so you can express it in a healthy way."

Brian and Thea's story profoundly illustrates how controlling, angry men can inflict deep pain on those they love. And I told it because Brian's hard work and Thea's eagerness to please him resulted in a redemptive ending. Over time Brian learned how to express his anger in a nondemanding way that recognized Thea's freedom. In the years that followed she made him very proud.

Thea learned to be open with her dad with the help of a counselor specializing in impulse control disorders. Once Brian understood her passion for art, he removed her from the public school she hated and enrolled her in an art prep school. She never took another math or language course and went on to study at the Art Institute of California. Her bedroom remained cluttered, but she no longer shoplifted. And because Brian kept his commitment to respect her freedom, he never verbally abused her again—even when he was furious with her.

TRUTHS TO LIVE BY

- I can't control another person, but I can control my anger.
- I should respect a person's freedom.
- Anger is sometimes an attempt to force others to conform to my own wishes.
- God doesn't impose his will on others, and neither should I.
- I must trust God to work in the lives of other people.
- I can give advice, but I can't control what people do with it.
- Discretion will make me slow to anger.

STRENGTHEN THE GOOD MAN

A man's discretion makes him slow to anger, and it is his glory to overlook a transgression. (PROVERBS 19:11, NASB)

People with understanding control their anger; a hot temper shows great foolishness. (PROVERBS 14:29)

DISCUSSION QUESTIONS

1. How do you respond when someone doesn't comply with your wishes—perhaps a child not doing chores, your wife not wanting sex, a fellow worker not following your instructions, or someone doing sloppy work that reflects poorly on you?

2. How do you express anger toward that person?

3. How does he or she generally respond to your anger?

4. How would you feel if someone got mad and yelled at you?

5. How do you use anger to try to force others to comply with your wishes?

6. How would it help you manage your anger if you recognized that other people are free and aren't obligated to conform to your wishes?

7. How could you use the principles of this chapter to help you express your anger in an assertive but respectful way?

8. How would meditating on Proverbs 19:11 help the good man in you express your anger as Jesus would?

CHAPTER 6

THE MAN WHO
WOULD BE GOD
Pride

JIM STRUTTED INTO my office with the cockiness of a mob boss. He was a successful pharmaceutical salesman known for his quick wit and faultless memory. Before sitting in the brown leather chair just in front of the windows, he pulled some lint out of his right pocket, rolled it into a ball, walked over to the fireplace, opened the glass doors, and flicked it onto the flames. He then picked up the Rubik's Cube I keep on my coffee table and twisted it without looking down. While playing with the toy, his feet tapped on the floor, keeping beat to a tune in his head. When he made no move to close the doors to the fireplace, I walked over and shut them.

As I watched his display of kinetic energy, he blurted out, "I've got problems with my wife, Chris. Last month she accused me of being a sex addict."

"Why would she do that?"

"Because I logged on to a porn site on the Internet."

"Does that happen often?"

"No, I'm not into porn," he said, tossing the Rubik's Cube onto the table and watching passively as it bounced off the table and fell to the floor. "I landed on the site because I typed in the wrong address. I thought it was funny, so I told her." He finally sat down in the leather chair.

"Why did you think it was funny?"

"Because I had mistyped a single letter, so instead of landing on a music site, I ended up on a porn site. The two names were identical except for one letter.

"Anyway, Chris freaked out big-time. She bought a book on sex addictions and convinced herself I was a sex addict. She started checking the browser history on my computer when I wasn't around. She reviewed the cable TV bills to see if I had ordered any porn. All of that annoyed me, but when she told our pastor, that infuriated me. I mean, I'm a leader in the church."

"Did you consider that she might have felt helpless?"

"Helpless? How about paranoid? How about controlling? How about nuts? Anyway, I didn't wait for our pastor to call me. I called him and let him know I've got my sexual appetite under control. I told him Chris is crazy and anytime she calls him with a concern to let me know."

"Did you and Chris talk through this?"

"We never talk through anything. Last month she thought I was a sex addict. This month she's convinced I'm a misogynist—you know, a man who hates women."

"Why does she think that?"

"She read some marriage book with a chapter about misogynists. The author offered a checklist to help readers determine if their husbands hate women. Being the brilliant amateur psychologist and all, she diagnosed me as a misogynist. I didn't even know what the word meant, and now I am one."

"Do you hate women?"

"Not at all," Jim said. Just then his cell phone vibrated. He pulled it out of his pocket and flipped it open. When he saw who was calling, he rolled his eyes, palmed the phone shut, and slid it back into his pocket. "In fact, when I told some of the women at the office what Chris had said, they laughed. You can talk to them if you want.

"I get along great with women," he added. "Well, except for Chris."

"How did you feel when she made those accusations?"

"I know she's unstable," he said, once again tapping his foot, "so I try to reason with her. I sit down and calmly walk her through why she's drawing faulty conclusions."

"How does she respond?"

"She gets mad and accuses me of not listening to her. I assure her I'm listening and prove it by reviewing everything she's said. The fact is, I remember the details of her babble better than she does."

"Have the two of you ever seen a counselor?"

"We've seen three counselors."

"Were they helpful?"

"They could have been. As long as the counselor talked about *my* issues, Chris was happy. But once the counselor began to zero in on Chris, she'd start crying or stop talking. She'd get upset and refuse to return."

"Why did you come to me?"

"So you could help us. I think Chris trusts you."

"Really? Even though I've never met her?"

"I've told her some of the counsel you've given me. She thinks you've got me figured out."

Since Jim and Chris had already seen three other counselors, I realized he probably would be more likely to buy a winning lottery ticket than get much help from me. But then I realized the couple might benefit more from several intensive counseling sessions than from many weekly sessions. "Jim, I'll meet with you and Chris, but only if you'll agree to four sessions of three hours each next week."

Jim surprised me with his willingness to adjust his schedule so we could meet so soon. The next Monday morning, the three of us met at my office. In spite of her failing marriage, Chris had a perkiness about her—a cheerfulness in her speech and a bounce in her step. Jim seemed more like a tugboat chugging along through choppy water. His head sat on a short neck and seemed as locked in place as a wheelhouse.

THE MAN WHO WAS NEVER WRONG

We had only been together a short time when they got into an argument about who was responsible for the empty gas tank in Jim's car.

"You drove it last, so it's *your* fault it was empty this morning," Jim said in a voice as calm and cold as an arctic breeze.

"I didn't drive your car yesterday. You did," Chris said with a hint of frustration.

"I brought it home and told you it was near empty. You then took it to the store and failed to put gas in it," Jim said.

"I took *my* car," Chris said. "Why would I take your car after you'd told me it was low on gas?"

Jim shook his head from side to side. While his voice stayed calm, the words came out rapid fire through a locked jaw. "I checked the odometer this morning. My car *had* been driven since I brought it home. No need for you to lie."

"I'm not lying," Chris said with a raised voice. "Did you consider that maybe one of the kids drove it? Besides, it doesn't matter. I filled it up this morning."

"Of course it doesn't matter to you. That's why you didn't fill it up yesterday like you promised. But it matters to me because I don't like driving the pickup to work. It's a piece of junk. You know . . ."

"I didn't drive your car, and I didn't promise to fill it up," Chris interjected with a flushed face and an even louder voice.

"Don't interrupt me," Jim said softly. "Let's talk this through politely. Please let me finish, and then you can talk."

"You're not letting me talk, and when I do you don't listen," she said, spitting the words in his direction.

"You don't need to get mad," Jim said. "I've heard every word you've said. I'm just pointing out that you're not being truthful and that it's your fault the car wasn't full this morning. "

As I listened to the argument, I noticed something important. While Jim maintained an even voice, his words seemed like poisoned darts zinging through the air. Upon impact they stung, contaminated, and killed.

17 percent of surveyed men usually express their anger by debating to prove their point.

I called a time-out and asked Jim if he didn't think his words were a bit harsh.

"Not at all," he said. "I'm under control. Chris is the one who's mad."

"Chris, did it hurt when he called you a liar?" I asked.

"Of course. But he talks like that all the time."

"I'm sorry if it hurt. But I'm only speaking the truth," Jim said.

I gazed at Jim for a moment. He honestly didn't realize the depth of the anger he felt toward Chris. And he didn't realize how spiteful his anger had become. "I'm not sure you are sorry," I said. "Your tone is controlled, but your words and demeanor are hostile."

Throughout the next two days I watched as Jim and Chris argued about a lost cell phone, their sex life, and their spending habits. Jim repeatedly hammered away at Chris with details proving he was right about every subject. He was speaking facts, while Chris was speaking feelings. At times he seemed like a robot talking to a human. And like an omniscient robot, he could make no mistakes about the data.

FACE-TO-FACE WITH PRIDE

Behind all of Jim's logic and attempts to prove he was right, I detected a spirit of pride. Not the healthy pride a father has when his son scores a touchdown or his daughter kicks a goal, but the kind of pride that nurtures arrogance and self-exaltation . . . the kind of pride that feeds the flesh, which in turn feeds anger.

Jim had no idea he wanted to be like God, but he definitely had a godlike view of himself. I suspect the process of taking the steps from mere mortal to the divine occurred so slowly and comfortably that he never noticed them.

As Jim talked *at* Chris, pride oozed from his pores. It

fluttered from his tongue. It emanated from his eyes. And it proved he had a problem more difficult to excise than a tumor wrapped around a carotid artery. A problem made more difficult because a man must admit to the problem before he can address it. I knew there was little chance I could convince Jim that he suffered from a severe case of arrogance.

Like bad breath, pride is easily sniffed out in others but almost impossible to detect in ourselves.

And then I had an idea I thought would bring Jim face-to-face with his pride.

The next day when Jim and Chris arrived, I pointed out the digital video recorder I wanted to use in our session.

Jim looked confused. "Why?"

"So you can both see how you come across to the other. Once you've viewed the recording and we've discussed it, I'll delete it. Are you okay with that?"

They agreed, and Chris even seemed to welcome the idea. After we reviewed what we had discussed on the previous days, I brought up the argument about the empty gas tank. Because it had never been resolved, I assumed the argument would begin at the same level of intensity it had ended at two days before. I wasn't disappointed. Jim's arrogance quickly took over, and he repeatedly accused Chris of lying and breaking her promise. Instead of refereeing, I sat back and let Jim's robotic character hammer away at Chris. After ten minutes I interrupted their banter and said we'd take a five-minute break and then watch the recording.

As we viewed the quarrel, I prayed God would open Jim's eyes so he would realize how he argued with a godlike authority. I wasn't sure what he was thinking because he sat silently in front of the monitor. And then suddenly he told me to turn off the recording; he had seen enough.

"Wow," Jim said. "I had no idea."

"What did you see?" I asked.

"I saw an angry, hard man speaking harsh words. I saw my pride and arrogance. I didn't even know I had an anger problem. Chris does all of the yelling, so I thought *she* was the angry person in our marriage."

"I get angry because you never listen to me," Chris said.

Before Jim could answer, I assured Chris we would be working on Jim's listening skills, but first we needed to deal with the underlying issue that prevented him from listening.

"I think it's pride that has blinded you, Jim."

"Pride is a hallucinogenic that causes a man to think he's God—the final authority on all topics . . . the one who doesn't need to apologize because he's never wrong. And since he's never wrong, he doesn't need to listen to others."

"Being right all the time is a terrible burden to bear," Jim said teasingly.

"But I'm the one carrying the burden," Chris said. "Not you."

PRIDE AND NARCISSISM

Of course, pride is an inherent part of the flesh. From the time we're born until we're about three to four years of age, each of us literally believes that we exist at the center of the universe. We live for one thing—having our wants and needs satisfied. We wish to be catered to—almost as if we were a god. As we get older, we begin to realize that we're mortal and only a tiny part of a large world. We eventually outgrow this natural selfishness as we discover that the needs of other people are as important to them as our needs are to us.

A very small percentage of people never outgrow the perception that they are divine and that their needs are the only ones that matter. Such people may have a perverted type of pride called narcissistic personality disorder (NPD). More often, as in Jim's case, they suffer from pride-driven narcissism. And a narcissistic man finds it hard to admit he's wrong. Acting with the authority of a god, he pushes others down by using guilt and shame.

"Have you noticed, Jim," I asked, "how often you use guilt and shame when you and Chris are arguing?"

"Do I?" he asked.

I nodded.

"Now that I've watched that tape," Jim said, "I guess I'd have to agree with you." He paused a moment. "But aren't guilt and shame the same thing?"

"No, they're not," I said. "Guilt is feeling bad about something you've done. Shame is feeling bad about who you are. You tried to lay guilt on Chris when you said it was her fault your car was out of gas. You shamed her when you said she was a liar.

Prideful, self-absorbed men think of themselves as superior and find pleasure in loading others down with guilt and shame."

"That pretty well sums up how Jim treats me," Chris said smugly.

"Okay," Jim said, clearly annoyed by her comment. "I get the message, Chris. Would you please back off? Besides, you've got your own issues with anger. At least I've never thrown anything at you."

"And when was the last time I did that?" Chris asked defiantly.

I used my hands to signal another time-out. "At some point the two of you need to call a truce," I said. "Maybe now would be a good time. Okay? You're both obsessed with putting each other down. Wouldn't you say that's an example of pride and self-centeredness?"

"I'd say that's true for Chris," Jim said jokingly.

"Definitely true for Jim," Chris retorted.

THE ORIGIN OF PRIDE

As we've seen, pride is a problem we all have. And because it's rooted in the flesh, our old man, it's crucial to understand it. When dominated by pride, Jim was no longer thinking and living out of his new and true identity in Christ. Instead, he'd fallen victim to the flesh and its self-serving and destructive anger. To overcome his pride, he had to understand its source.

With that thought in mind, I directed Jim and Chris to two passages that tell us about Satan's pride-induced fall. First, I read Isaiah 14:12-14 aloud:

How you are fallen from heaven,
   O shining star, son of the morning!
You have been thrown down to the earth,
   you who destroyed the nations of the world.

For you said to yourself,
      "I will ascend to heaven and set my throne above
         God's stars.
   I will preside on the mountain of the gods
      far away in the north.
   I will climb to the highest heavens
      and be like the Most High."

Next, we looked at Ezekiel 28:17:

Your heart was filled with pride
   because of all your beauty.
Your wisdom was corrupted
   by your love of splendor.
So I threw you to the ground
   and exposed you to the curious gaze of kings.

"Since pride puffed up Satan's heart and prompted him to seek God's throne," I said, "it's no surprise he tempted Eve with the promise that she, too, could become like God. Satan deceived her into believing that if she would take one bite of the forbidden fruit, her eyes would be opened and she would be like God, knowing good and evil.

"When Satan spoke to Eve, Adam stood right beside her and failed to correct the lie.[1] With one bite, he, too, sinned, and with sin came pride. This same sinful nature was passed down to his descendants. It didn't take long for pride to turn into murderous anger. Adam and Eve's firstborn son, Cain, got angry and killed his brother after God rejected his grain offering but accepted Abel's animal sacrifice.[2]

"God had told Cain that he must master the sin that was crouching at his door. Unfortunately, he didn't obey. But we can."

"Honestly, Bill, I've never considered whether or not I'm arrogant," Jim said. "Dealing with pride seems about as easy as grabbing air. You know it's there, but you can't see it."

"That's a good analogy," I said.

> **"Getting rid of pride is like removing air from a glass. The easiest way would be to fill the glass with water. In order to evict pride we must replace it with humility."**

HOW TO CULTIVATE HUMILITY

"I've never met a man who said the area of greatest growth in his life has been in the area of humility," I noted. "Who would say, 'I used to be proud, but now I'm humble'?"

Jim and Chris laughed. They appeared more relaxed.

"A lot of guys think a humble man is a wimp who lets others push him around. That's not true," I said. "A humble man is one who has an accurate view of himself. He recognizes his own weaknesses and need for God's grace."

I pulled out an index card on which I'd written several verses for Jim to begin meditating on:

*The LORD supports the humble, but he brings the
wicked down into the dust.* (PSALM 147:6)
*The LORD mocks the mockers but is gracious to the
humble.* (PROVERBS 3:34)
*God blesses those who are poor and realize their need
for him, for the Kingdom of Heaven is theirs.*
(MATTHEW 5:3)

Before reading the final verse aloud, I pointed out that even
Jesus, the Lord of the universe, defined himself as humble:

I am humble and gentle at heart. (MATTHEW 11:29)

STRENGTHEN THE NEW MAN

"Because I've struggled with arrogance myself," I told Jim, "I've
thought a lot about how to develop humility. I've decided we
have two choices. One way is to do nothing and wait for God
to humble us. Scripture tells us that God tears down the proud
man's house.³

"That verse reminds me of the story of the woodpecker that
was banging away on a tree when a bolt of lightning hit the
tree and split it in half. The bird flew away, looked over his
shoulder, and told a friend, 'Look what I did.' No sooner had
the words left his beak than a bolt of lightning knocked him
out of the sky.

"Whenever I sense I'm impressed with myself it scares me,"
I said, "because I know if I don't deal with my attitude, God
will. Not with a bolt of lightning but with a dose of reality to
deflate my ballooned ego."

"So what's the second way of dealing with pride?" Jim asked.

"The second, less painful way involves two steps that strengthen the new man. The first step involves considering how we think and speak. Solomon was pretty clear about that," I said, as I paged through my Bible to Proverbs 27:2. "'Let someone else praise you, not your own mouth—a stranger, not your own lips,'" I read.

"The crucial point here is that our words reveal our thoughts. A man who praises himself puts his thoughts on display. Jesus says, 'For whatever is in your heart determines what you say.'[4] A person who continually talks himself up—or puts himself down, for that matter—is self-focused and arrogant."

"How would putting himself down show a man's arrogance?" Jim asked.

"A humble man sees himself as he really is before God and other people. Even when he's done something wrong or failed miserably, he knows he has value. If, instead, he claims he's worse than everyone else, he's actually lifting himself above God and saying, 'I can determine my worth better than God can. God says I have value, but he's wrong.' That kind of pride also fuels anger.

"Of course, the man who constantly brags or fishes for compliments reveals another side of pride. He has an insatiable appetite for more praise, both from himself and others.

"So step one in cultivating humility involves listening to your own words," I said. "Ask yourself, 'Am I praising myself or putting myself down? Am I fishing for compliments?'"

The secret to right thinking, I told Jim and Chris, is found in Psalm 1:1-2, where David says:

Oh, the joys of those who do not
follow the advice of the wicked,

> *or stand around with sinners,*
> *or join in with mockers.*

> *But they delight in the law of the LORD,*
> *meditating on it day and night.*

"The more we meditate on God's Word," I said, "the more we see ourselves as we truly are. Such thinking creates humility and nurtures the new man in us. Jim, this is how we begin to develop godliness and humility and manage our anger."

OBEY GOD: PUT OTHERS FIRST

"That sounds like a tall order," said Jim.

"It is," I agreed. "In fact, it's impossible without God's help. The apostle Paul illustrated how difficult it is by describing the selfless humility Jesus demonstrated while on earth. Why don't we turn to the book of Philippians for a minute?" I said.

I flipped to this letter from Paul and, after finding the passage I was thinking of, said, "Here it is. Philippians 2:3-8. Listen to what Paul says:

> *Don't be selfish; don't try to impress others. Be humble,*
> *thinking of others as better than yourselves. Don't look*
> *out only for your own interests, but take an interest in*
> *others, too.*

> *You must have the same attitude that Christ Jesus had.*

> *Though he was God,*
> *he did not think of equality with God*

> *as something to cling to.*
> *Instead, he gave up his divine privileges;*
> *he took the humble position of a slave*
> *and was born as a human being.*
> *When he appeared in human form,*
> *he humbled himself in obedience to God*
> *and died a criminal's death on a cross.*

"See how Paul urged the Philippians to demonstrate humility by considering the interests of others before their own, just like Jesus? What I find fascinating about this passage is that Jesus humbled himself by obeying his Father . . . even when such obedience resulted in his suffering on a cross.

"Instead of serving the pride that resides in our old man, the flesh, we're to obey God and serve others. That means that every time I'm angry, I should ask myself, *What does God want me to do? How can I use my anger to serve others?*"

ANGER SLOWLY; RECOVER QUICKLY

Jim spoke up. "This is all very interesting," he said, "but how do I know what God wants me to do with my anger?"

"Great question," I said. "I can think of two key directives we must obey. The Bible tells us to be slow to anger. And Paul advises us to process our anger quickly so we don't give the devil an opportunity to lead us into sin.[5]"

"Get angry slowly and recover quickly," Jim noted.

"Right," I said. "Unlike God, we can't always discern if the wrong we're observing is a real wrong or a perceived wrong. That's why we need to be slow to get angry. Making such an admission will be difficult for you, Jim, because you tend to

believe you're always right and that your anger is always justified. Your pride fuels that error in thinking."

*43 percent of surveyed men have
no plan to help them process and
express their anger in a healthy way.*

"So how do I correct it?"

"You've got to teach yourself to be slow to anger by thinking clearly when you're first getting angry. Anger is often triggered when a man feels disrespected. His pride prompts him
to defend himself and set the record straight. It's crucial at that
moment for him to tap into his new and true identity in Christ.
He must not allow his pride to intensify his anger. When this
happens to you, you need to pause and allow the true you, the
new you in Christ, to think, *Is my anger justified? How can I use
my anger to help others?*

"If you can't process your anger that fast, say nothing and
get away from the situation. And then instead of reviewing how
you've been wronged, which will feed your pride and flesh,
think through the situation from the other person's point of
view. Only then, after you've processed your anger, should you
talk with the person who angered you. Remember, most of the
time if you speak when angry, you'll regret what you say."

ANGER TUNE-UP

The advantage of four days of intensive counseling is that it
allows an individual or couple to gain life-changing insights
and to quickly put an effective game plan into place. The

digital recording triggered such a dramatic paradigm shift in Jim's thinking that he requested a copy for future review. After the four sessions, Jim and I met weekly for a few months to talk about his progress. As he focused on cultivating humility he listened better, demanded less, and managed his anger more effectively.

I also met with Chris for several months to help her learn to support Jim, without trying to monitor and control his behavior. We also talked about how she could best respond to Jim if she detected he was expressing his anger in a harmful way (I'll tell her story in chapter nine).

Two years after our sessions, Jim called me one day. "Bill, it's me. I'd like you and Cindy to join Chris and me for a three-day intensive."

Confused, I asked him what he had in mind.

"I'd like us to go on a scuba diving trip. We could dive in the mornings and talk in the afternoons. I ran it by Chris, and she thinks it's a great way to justify a vacation. What do you think?"

"Jim, I can either be your counselor/coach or your friend. I can't be both. Which do you want me to be?"

"How about this," Jim said. "When we dive you'll be my friend, and then during the intensives, you and Cindy can coach us—as friends."

I didn't have to think too long about his offer. "I think it may be a good time to do another intensive. But it needs to be someplace warm," I joked.

And so that winter the four of us made the trip to Cozumel. And amazingly, Jim and Chris didn't get in a single argument—

at least any that were fueled by uncontrolled anger. Now Jim argued like a man . . . not a man who would be God.[6]

TRUTHS TO LIVE BY

- Pride feeds my flesh, which in turn feeds my anger.
- An arrogant man believes he's always right.
- A narcissistic man is preoccupied with himself and lacks empathy.
- Arrogant men act with the assumed authority of God and push others down with guilt and shame.
- A humble man processes and expresses his anger in a godly way.
- A humble man gains an accurate view of himself by meditating on God's Word.
- A humble man considers others more important than himself.
- I cultivate humility with controlled thoughts and words.
- I cultivate humility through obedience to God.

STRENGTHEN THE GOOD MAN

Don't be selfish; don't try to impress others. Be humble, thinking of others as better than yourselves. Don't look out only for your own interests, but take an interest in others, too. (PHILIPPIANS 2:3-4)

The LORD sustains the humble but casts the wicked to the ground. (PSALM 147:6, NIV)

DISCUSSION QUESTIONS

1. When have you felt healthy pride for yourself or someone else?

2. What characterizes an arrogant and prideful man? In what ways does he act like he thinks he's God?

3. How does pride fuel the flesh? How does pride fuel anger?

4. How does pride prevent a man from processing his anger in a healthy way?

5. Why is the pursuit of humility the best way to overcome pride?

6. Read Philippians 2:1-11. How did Jesus demonstrate humility? How can you follow his example?

7. How can you get angry slowly and recover from anger quickly?

8. What two things will you do this week to cultivate humility so you can more effectively manage and express your anger?

CHAPTER 7

THE MAN WHO BURIED HIS WIFE ALIVE

Forgiveness

THE IDEA OF burying his wife alive appealed to Stephen, not as a first option, but as a final one . . . one he hoped would enable him to break away from the past and step into the future. When you discover how he accomplished this, you'll realize things are not as they initially appear and words do not always mean what they seem to say.

In a sense, that's why Stephen came to see me the first time. After months of grueling business travel, he was finally relaxing with his family during a much-needed vacation when everything went wrong. Or, worse still, he discovered that everything had been wrong for some time and he hadn't realized it.

At the time we met I was leading a church in Houston. My office had a lovely view of a hospital, a parking lot, and some commercially operated batting cages. What it lacked in a view it made up for with wood paneling on the walls, a mahogany desk where I studied, and a sitting area with a tan love seat and matching chair.

Stephen had been referred to me by a friend of his. When he entered my office, he looked deeply troubled. After we shook hands and were seated, I asked him if everything was okay.

"No, everything is not okay," he said.

"What's happened?" I asked.

Stephen cleared his throat and rubbed his chin with the fingers of his left hand. He then leaned toward me and said, "My wife, Heidi, our eight-year-old son, Blake, and I were at a resort in Colorado. You know, one of those ranch-type places where we could fish, bike, ride horses, and relax. We loved the location because it gave us a break from the heat and humidity of Houston. The lodge sat in a grass-covered valley surrounded by towering mountain peaks. Because it was early summer, we could still see snow at the higher elevations. Our cabin was in a secluded spot in the midst of a growth of ponderosa pines. There was a small brook beside it. The fragrance of the trees and the sound of the stream created an idyllic setting.

"One morning Heidi went for a bike ride with Blake, and I stayed at the cabin. I poured myself a mug of coffee and looked for a book I had brought to read on the trip. I spotted it on the table beside the bed. As I reached for it, I noticed something else—Heidi's journal. I'm not sure why I picked it up. I'd never even glanced at her journal before. Doing so seemed like an invasion of privacy. And I figured we all need privacy, even in marriage. Looking back, I think it was God who prompted me to open it.

"I randomly opened it to no page in particular. I hadn't read more than a few sentences when my gut turned sour and my chest constricted. I literally ran to the bathroom, where I bent over the toilet and threw up."

THE GREAT LIE

"I returned to the journal and read page after page after page. Stunned, I walked to the side of the house, climbed on a bike, and searched for Heidi and Blake. I found them sitting on a bench by a pond. I rode up to Heidi, looked her in the eyes, and said, 'I've read your journal. I know what you've done.' I then pedaled back to the cabin."

"What did she say?" I asked.

"It was weird. She just nodded. She didn't look shocked or angry. I guess she looked resigned."

"Did she follow you back to the cabin?"

"No. She didn't return for a couple of hours. It was after noon, and she had dropped Blake off at the horse stable to go on an afternoon ride so we could be alone. I didn't wait for her to say anything. Instead I asked if what she had written was a fantasy. I guess I was in denial. I didn't want what I had read to be true. I wanted an explanation that I could live with . . . something without pain. I hoped she had been trying to write a romance novel."

"That must have been a horrible moment," I said. "I mean when you asked her that question."

"I felt like I was standing inside a bubble that was suspended in time. I heard the clock on the fireplace mantel slowly tap out a single second. Through the open windows I heard the wind blow through the pine trees."

"And then Heidi spoke and the bubble burst. 'I wish it were a fantasy,' she said. 'But it's not. It's true. I'm sorry.'"

"Were you angry?" I asked.

"At the moment I felt only pain. But the pain would turn into anger soon enough. And I'm not just mad at Heidi."

"You must be mad at the other guy," I said.

"Of course I'm mad at him. But then there's Heidi's friend. She knew but never mentioned it to me. And there are the two counselors she met with who didn't tell me—including one we'd been seeing together. She even told one of the pastors at our church, and he never told me. I felt like they had all deceived me."

"Are you mad at yourself?"

"Yeah. A year ago I suspected something was going on. Heidi was exercising and getting in shape. She looked great. My gut said something was wrong. I kiddingly asked Heidi if she was having an affair. She assured me I was the only man in her life."

"How are you going to deal with your anger?" I asked.

Stephen gazed at me for several seconds. "I don't know. But I do know my anger could destroy me and any hope I have of rebuilding my marriage."

"That's a crucial admission," I said. "Are you up to taking some difficult steps in processing your anger?"

"I hope so."

"You need to meet with each of the people you're angry with."

"I've already talked with one of them," he said. "The guy already called me. He wanted me to know he's not a monster. He said he was sorry."

"How did you respond?"

"I told him I forgave him. And I did."

"What did he say?"

"He pleaded with me to yell at him. He asked me to tell him what a slimeball I thought he was. I told him I didn't feel that way because I had forgiven him. Actually, I haven't blamed him. I'm not married to him; I'm married to Heidi."

"You need to talk with the other people," I said, picking up a Bible. I read aloud Jesus' words in Matthew 18:15:

> **"If another believer sins against you, go**
> **privately and point out the offense. If**
> **the other person listens and confesses**
> **it, you have won that person back."**

LEARNING TO FORGIVE

The next week Stephen and I met again. He reported that he had talked with his pastor, Heidi's friend, and the counselor who'd been meeting with both him and Heidi. The pastor said he had given Heidi a deadline to tell Stephen. He said he told her if she didn't meet it, he would tell Stephen himself. Her friend made no apology and said she had to keep Heidi's secret. She insisted she was helping Heidi work through the situation.

The counselor explained to Stephen that the law mandated he maintain the confidentiality of a client. Stephen rejected that explanation and asked the counselor how he could, with a clear conscience, take his money and never tell him, or have Heidi tell him, the truth.

"Okay, you've met with each of them," I said. "Was it helpful?"

"It helped some, I guess. I still feel they weren't honest with me about Heidi. I feel better after listening to their point of view, but I wish they had told me the truth."

46 percent of surveyed men
identified dishonesty as the leading
cause of anger for them.

"Do you think the counselor should have violated Heidi's confidence?"

"No. But I think he should either have told her to tell me or stopped seeing us."

"Will you forgive him?"

"I forgive him, yes. But I still think he's a jerk, and I'd never refer anyone to him. I wish I could get a refund."

"How are things going with Heidi?"

"Sometimes I get toxic images of her with the other guy. I've begged God to take away those thoughts. The other night, after Heidi and Blake had gone to bed, I sat in front of the TV trying to unwind. After hearing a late-night comic joking about wives who cheat on their inattentive husbands, I lost it. I took off my wedding ring, walked to the garage, found a hammer, and smashed the ring. I then placed it on the bathroom counter by Heidi's sink with a note that said, 'This is what I think of our wedding vows.'"

"That's a powerful message."

"It's how I feel," Stephen said.

"What did she say when she saw the note and ring?"

"She said she didn't blame me. The next morning while she was in the shower, I pulled all of her clothes out of her dresser and closet and threw them on the bed. I was cramming them into black plastic trash bags when she entered the room.

"She asked what I was doing. I told her I hated her and wanted her out of the house. She refused to leave . . . said I was hurt and she understood."

"What did you say?"

"I didn't say anything. I just left. I climbed in the car and drove to the gym. When I returned she had put her clothes back. I told her if she wasn't going to leave permanently, I wanted her to leave for the day and take Blake with her."

"Why did you say that?"

"I'm not sure."

"What were you feeling when you crushed your wedding ring and then threw her clothes into the bags and told her to leave?"

Stephen paused for several seconds as he pondered how to answer. "I felt powerful. Anger is a strong emotion, and when I turn it loose it feels good. I can use it to destroy things, like my ring, or to hurt people, like Heidi. It gives me a sense of control."

"So did you tell her to leave for the day to exert control over her or to avoid hurting her?"

"I guess it was both. I wanted to control her, but I also wanted to vent my anger without worrying about saying something I'd regret. I didn't want to hurt her or Blake. And I wanted time alone with God."

"Did she leave?"

"Yeah, she and Blake left. I spent the rest of the day alone and did a lot of thinking and praying. I especially thought about how she ended up in such a dark place."

"Did you come up with anything that helped you understand her?"

"We talked about it when she got back," Stephen said. "I think it's pretty simple, really. She had some painful childhood experiences. But I'm not sure how knowing about her past will help me forgive her. I think it would help if the two of us met with you," Stephen said.

CULTIVATE COMPASSION

Over the years I've learned that nothing fuels anger like an unwillingness to forgive a wrong suffered . . . especially when the wrong involves betrayal and humiliation. Stephen suffered both and was understandably struggling to forgive his wife so he could effectively process and manage his anger. His suggestion that the three of us meet was crucial because in order to forgive he would need to understand why his wife ended up in the arms of another man. While no explanation would justify such betrayal, it would at least help Stephen along the path of forgiveness by helping him cultivate compassion instead of bitterness.

*23 percent of surveyed men said they
seldom or never feel compassion
toward someone they're angry with.*

51 percent said they sometimes do.

24 percent said they often do.

When we met a week later, Heidi didn't waste any time getting to the point. "I have no excuse for what I did," she said. "But I think I understand how it happened. To begin with, I have a hard time trusting men. When I was a child, my dad abandoned my mom and me. A few years later my mother married a wonderful man who treated me like a princess. He played with me. He bought gifts for me. He helped me with my homework. And then when I was twelve, he died in a car wreck. The two most important men in my life left, and they never came back.

"When Stephen and I fell in love and got married, I always feared he, too, would leave me. Because of that I flirted with other men. I didn't want another relationship; I just needed to know that if Stephen ever left, I could find someone else.

"When we moved from Nashville to Houston I had no support system. My friends were back in Tennessee, and Stephen was working all the time. We started attending a church nearby, but because Stephen traveled most weekends, I usually went alone. One Sunday I met Brad, a divorcé. I flirted with him. He flirted back. The next week, after I dropped Blake off at children's church, I saw Brad in the lobby. He asked me to skip church and join him for brunch.

"In that moment I knew I should turn him down. Instead I made the biggest mistake of my life."

"Was the affair ongoing?" I asked.

"No. It was sporadic. By the time Stephen read my journal, it was over. Brad and I hadn't seen each other for three months."

"Why didn't you tell me?" Stephen asked.

Heidi gazed at Stephen as her eyes filled with tears. "I was afraid you'd leave me. I hated myself and couldn't imagine that you wouldn't hate me too."

Stephen listened silently.

"Do you hate her?" I asked.

He shook his head from side to side and looked at Heidi. "I forgive you," he said. "But I'm still hurting, and I'm still angry."

CHOOSE FORGIVENESS

"What do you mean when you say that you forgive her?" I asked.

"I mean that I choose not to hold what she did against her. I'm hurting and I'm still angry, but I believe that with the help of God I can love her.

"It's helped that she hasn't defended herself," he continued. "And it's helped that when I'm angry she has absorbed it rather than retaliating."

> *57 percent of surveyed men said that if their wives had an affair they would forgive them and try to work through it.*
>
> *32 percent said they didn't know what they would do.*
>
> *7 percent said they would end the marriage.*

Stephen then said something to Heidi that stunned me. "I respect you more now than before."

Heidi shook her head in disbelief. "How could you?"

"Because while you did something terribly wrong, you've

owned it and you're doing everything I need you to do to help me get past this."

Turning to me, Stephen then asked, "But how do I get past it? How do I get past the terrible images in my mind? It feels good to review them and then to contemplate how I can get back at Heidi. I enjoy nursing bitterness because the bitterness fuels my anger, which seems to give me the power to get even."

NURTURE THE NEW YOU IN TWO WAYS

I knew there was no quick fix for Stephen's emotional wound. And I knew that any advice I'd give might sound like I was offering an aspirin to someone with a brain tumor. "Stephen, you're a new and good man in Christ. But your flesh, the old man in you, feeds off evil and spiteful images and thoughts. The good news is that you don't have to allow your old man to control your thoughts. You must choose to focus your mental energy on positive and healthy thoughts."

FIRST: CHOOSE POSITIVE THOUGHTS

I walked over to my bookshelf and pulled down three Bibles. I handed one to Stephen, one to Heidi, and I kept one for myself. I asked them to turn to Philippians 4:8, where Paul says,

And now, dear brothers and sisters, one final thing. Fix your thoughts on what is true, and honorable, and right, and pure, and lovely, and admirable. Think about things that are excellent and worthy of praise.

After we had read the passage I told them, "I once met with a man to discuss a terrible wrong he had suffered from a business partner. He wanted to know how he could ever forgive such an act of betrayal. I told him he needed to do two things. He laughed and said forgiveness couldn't possibly be that simple. I told him it was a simple prescription but not an easy one to administer."

"What did you tell him?" Stephen asked.

"I told him that every time he thought about his friend he needed to think something positive about this person and thank God for that trait or a past deed. When I mentioned earlier that your flesh feeds off of evil and spiteful images, what I meant was that, in the case of that businessman, every time he reviewed how he had been wronged it nurtured his old man and strengthened his sinful flesh. Soon his flesh, filled with bitterness and hatred, controlled his thoughts and emotions. He had become a slave to sin and saw no path to freedom. That's why, in order to forgive the guy who wronged him, that businessman had to replace spiteful images with positive ones."

SECOND: PRAY POSITIVE PRAYERS

"The second thing he needed to do was pray for his business partner. And I emphasized that he couldn't pray that God would zap him with a bolt of lightning. Instead, he needed to pray that God would bring something good into his life."

I then had Stephen and Heidi turn to Matthew 5:44-45 where Jesus says, "But I say, love your enemies! Pray for those who persecute you! In that way, you will be acting as true children of your Father in heaven. For he gives his sunlight to both the evil and the good, and he sends rain on the just and the unjust alike."

I told Stephen and Heidi, "My advice to that man was based on this command of Jesus, who told us to pray for those who wrong us. I told him that as a new man in Christ, he was a son of God. And just as his heavenly Father blesses evil men with sunshine and rain, so he should pray God's blessing on the man who wronged him."

*38 percent of surveyed men usually
or occasionally process and express
their anger in a healthy way.*

"Did he agree to give it a try?" Stephen asked.

"Not initially," I said. "He told me he hated the guy and couldn't think of anything positive about him. He said he would not pray God's blessing on his life. When we met a few weeks later, he told me he needed to confess something to me. I feared the worst. But I didn't need to. He said that a few days after our last meeting he had decided to give my suggestion a try."

"'At first my flesh fought me tooth and nail,'" he told me. "'It did not want me to think positively about that scoundrel. And praying for God's blessing on his life seemed impossible. But I ignored the pull of my flesh and remembered some good things he had done for me in the past. Every time I thought of him I thanked God for those good deeds. And I prayed God would strengthen his marriage and his business decisions.'

"The guy was astounded when his feelings for his business partner began to change. I really wasn't surprised."

**"I'm convinced bitterness and love
can't grow in the same heart."**

"If you choose to foster positive thoughts about Heidi and pray for God's blessing on her life, the painful memories will begin to fade. It won't happen overnight because you've been deeply hurt. But you will begin to heal. And as you heal, your anger will subside.

"As you pray for Heidi, ask God to assure her of both his love and yours. She said it was a fear of abandonment that prompted her to flirt in the first place. More than ever she needs to know that you still love her and will be there for her. As you focus on loving her—in spite of her betrayal—it will become easier to forgive her."

"But I'm having a hard time forgiving myself," Stephen said. "I feel so stupid. My gut told me Heidi was messing around, and I ignored it."

"Stephen," Heidi said, "you're not stupid. You trusted me, and I lied to you. I covered my tracks. None of this is your fault."

"The affair was your bad choice," Stephen said. "But the fact that I neglected you after we moved to Houston was my fault. If I had stayed home and given you more attention, you wouldn't have been in such a vulnerable place."

"It's good that you recognize that," I said. "In the future, instead of punishing yourself for your past failures, thank God that he has shown you how you can love Heidi in a way that makes her feel secure and treasured. Ask him to enable you to assure her of your love . . . even when you're hurting."

As our time wound down, I reminded Stephen of his two-step assignment: (1) to thank God for something about Heidi every time he thought of her, and (2) to pray God's blessing on specific areas of her life.

BURIED AT THE BEACH

The following week when Stephen and I met, he made a painful admission. "I feel like my first marriage has died."

"What do you mean?" I asked.

"I mean prior to the affair I had all of these unrealistic and naive beliefs about Heidi and our marriage. I thought we would live happily ever after. I thought that since we both knew Christ he would protect us from serious harm.

"And I know God's not responsible for our sin, but still . . . I just thought nothing like this would happen to us. I saw Heidi as insecure but morally strong. I saw myself as an easygoing guy who didn't hold grudges. I thought anger was a problem other men struggled with. I even felt superior to men with marital problems. All of that is dead. I'm not sure where to go from here. Hopefully this weekend will help."

"What's going on this weekend?" I asked.

"I'll tell you about it when I get back."

When we met the next week Stephen made a statement that stunned me.

"I buried Heidi alive," he said with an eerie calmness.

"You did what?" I asked, imagining Heidi's dead body buried under six feet of dirt in Stephen's backyard.

"Let me explain," he said. "Heidi and I went to Galveston to celebrate our tenth wedding anniversary. We left Blake at a friend's house.

"As you know, summers at the Texas coast are hot and humid. The sand is so hot that even crabs scamper across it quickly to avoid searing their claws. But last weekend the November air was crisp and inviting. An hour before sunset we sat on a porch swing watching the waves break onto the beach. Then I asked Heidi to walk with me to the water's edge. A moment later our feet sank into the soft sand and we left a trail of prints to mark our path. She never asked me about the shovel and beach bag I carried.

"Soon white froth, the remnants of waves, washed over our feet. I turned and faced the beach house. And then I took ten large steps away from the waves, counting loudly as I took each one. When I stopped, she asked me what I was doing.

"I told her, 'Each step stands for one year of our marriage.'

"I then took a tape measure out of the beach bag and handed it to her. While she watched I placed my right foot on the top lip of the shovel head and stepped down on it. A moment later I removed a shovelful of sand. 'How deep is it?' I asked.

"She measured the depth using the tape measure. 'Six inches,' she said.

"I removed a bit more sand and she measured again. 'Ten inches,' she said.

"'One inch for each year of our marriage,' I said.

"I then took from the beach bag an envelope into which I had placed a picture of our wedding, a picture of Heidi, a picture of me, a copy of our marriage certificate, and a piece of paper on which I had written everything about our marriage that I believed had died when she had the affair. I handed Heidi the envelope. She took everything out and gently stroked each picture and read the list.

"When she had finished I pulled a notepad and pen from the beach bag and asked her to write out all of the things she thought had died when she had the affair. She began to cry. Slowly she made her list. I read it and wept with her.

"I remember hearing a seagull's cry and feeling the salt-filled wind blowing off the water. 'I'm burying you and me alive in this envelope,' I said. 'I'm burying our marriage, our hopes, our dreams, our sins, and our lists.'

"I placed the envelope in the grave and covered it with sand. 'Our new marriage will be better,' I said. 'It won't be the first one because it's now dead. But it will be better because it's based on failure and forgiveness.'

"Heidi was still crying, so I held her for a long time. Then I pulled from my pocket a chain of gold that held a golden heart. I held it up for her to see. 'Do you know what this is?' I asked her.

"'A necklace,' she said, fingering the heart.

"'Do you remember when I smashed my wedding ring?'

"'I remember,' she said.

"And then she realized what I had done. 'This is your ring,' she said as she wrapped her arms around me and squeezed. I had never been held by a resurrected woman before."

TRUTHS TO LIVE BY

- It's easier to forgive someone I understand.
- I will process my anger alone with God.
- I will cultivate forgiveness by cultivating compassion.
- Forgiveness is my choice.
- I will nurture the new and good me by choosing positive thoughts.
- I will nurture the new and good me by praying positive prayers.
- I will bury the past so I can celebrate the future.

STRENGTHEN THE GOOD MAN

If another believer sins against you, go privately and point out the offense. If the other person listens and confesses it, you have won that person back. (MATTHEW 18:15)

And now, dear brothers and sisters, one final thing. Fix your thoughts on what is true, and honorable, and right, and pure, and lovely, and admirable. Think about things that are excellent and worthy of praise. (PHILIPPIANS 4:8)

DISCUSSION QUESTIONS

1. How have you suffered betrayal in the past?

2. How have past wrongs fed your anger?

3. Why is forgiveness important for a man who wants to manage and express his anger in a godly way?

4. In Matthew 5:44-48, how does Jesus tell us to deal with our enemies?

5. Why is it important to spend some time processing our anger alone with God?

6. How can you cultivate compassion for those who have wronged you?

7. In what way is forgiveness a choice?

8. What two things can you do to nurture the new you so that you'll be able to extend forgiveness to someone who has hurt you?

CHAPTER 8

THE MAN ACCUSED OF STEALING FROM HIS DAD

Blessing

"I DREAMED ABOUT my dad last night," Joel said.

Whenever someone begins a counseling session with a comment like that, he's got my attention. It's not that I interpret dreams, but dreams may reveal what's happening in a man's soul. "Do you dream about him often?" I asked.

"Yes. The first year after his death the dreams tormented me. I'd wake up angry. The dreams opened old wounds that oozed bitterness."

Joel was tall and muscular with an angular face and a full head of black hair that he combed straight back. His brown eyes could either unsettle or relax someone depending on his intent. As he spoke about his father, he seemed sad, and his sadness enveloped the room as if a cloud had suddenly descended on us.

"How did your dad hurt you?" I asked.

"My dad was an angry man," Joel said.

He paused after that statement as though it had hurt him to make it. And then he reflected for a moment, searching for what to say next. "I asked his sister once about his childhood. She told me that my grandfather, whom I met only once, used to beat my dad when he misbehaved. That didn't surprise me," Joel said. "And then she told me something that could have come out of a horror movie. She said my grandfather would beat my dad whenever his older brother, Jack, would misbehave."

"Why would he do that?"

"My dad used to beat up his older brother. That would have been bad enough, but Jack was my grandfather's favorite child. The beatings were intended to teach my dad how it felt to be bullied."

"So Jack never got punished?"

"Not according to my aunt.

"When my dad was fifteen he decided not to take the abuse anymore. One day his father started to beat him with a belt. Dad stood up to him, grabbed the belt, and threatened to beat him unconscious if he ever touched him again. My dad left home that day and never returned."

53 percent of surveyed men rated their relationships with their fathers as excellent or good.

27 percent said they were terrible or poor.

"No wonder he was angry," I said.

"He left Montana and moved to Texas, where he worked in the oil fields," Joel said. "He wed a young woman—actually, it was my mom's older sister—and when my mother was fifteen he got her (my mother, not his wife) pregnant. He was twenty-four at the time. He said it was Mother's fault for climbing into bed with him. Two years later they had another child. Eventually he divorced his wife and married my mother. They had another girl and a son. I was the son.

"My dad realized he could make more money in sales than from working in the fields, so he launched a business that provided oil companies with pipe and heavy equipment. He made a lot of money, but he also made a lot of bad investments. And every time he believed somebody had wronged him. He never forgot a wrong suffered, and he spent a lot of time thinking and talking about how he had been swindled by his friends."

"How did he express anger?" I asked.

"When I was a boy I remember him slapping Mother a few times when they had both been drinking. For the most part they would yell at each other. In his old age he just talked about how he had been cheated by his friends and cheated on by my mother.

"As Mother grew older, she became frail. Then my dad got pretty sick, and she couldn't give him the care he needed. When he had to move in with us, he resented my mom for not taking care of him. He felt like he had supported her all of her life, and now in his old age she had kicked him out. He didn't want to leave Texas, and he resented me, even though I was glad to share my home with him."

"Why did he resent you?"

As he tilted his head, he seemed to search for what to say. "Dad used to make sarcastic remarks about his small bedroom. He would have preferred the master suite, but Sue never would have gone for that. And he resented the fact that I didn't try to talk Mother into keeping him with her."

Joel leaned forward as though a slow leak had deflated his

body. He then inhaled and sat back up. "One day Dad called me into his room. He was sitting at his desk and pulled a set of keys out of the drawer. He tossed them to me. No sooner had I caught them than he handed me a piece of paper. He told me they were the keys and title to his restored 1956 Thunderbird convertible. He had given me his most prized possession . . . said he wanted me to enjoy it while he was still alive."

"That was generous," I said.

"Yeah, I thought so too," Joel said.

His words sounded flat, and I knew the story would not end well.

"A month later I heard Dad talking on the phone to one of my sisters. He told her I had stolen his car. He said I had snuck the title out of his safety deposit box and forged his signature. He insisted I couldn't wait for him to die . . . I had to have the car now.

"When he hung up I asked him why he had said that. He said he just wanted her to know what kind of a man I really was."

"Did he forget that he had given it to you?"

"No. When I offered to transfer the title back to his name, he told me to keep it. He said he had given it to me. But he told a lot of people I had stolen the car from him, and some of them believed him. His anger made him mean."

"You said after his death dreams about him tormented you. Has that changed?"

"It's been five years, and it's different now. I'll dream about throwing a baseball with him or watching a football game. Once I dreamed we were working on the Thunderbird together. I've forgiven him."

"It sounds like you loved him."

"I still do," Joel said. "While he was angry and sometimes mean, he was my boyhood hero. He coached my baseball and football teams.

"I remember the day I learned I would never become the man he wanted me to be. He assumed I would take over his company one day, but I had no interest in the oil business. I was in high school, and we talked about my future. When he found out I wanted to go to college and law school, he turned cruel. I had just decided to play golf instead of football, and he brought that up. He said golf was for kids who couldn't make it in real sports. He said I was a loser and always would be."

"Did he ever apologize?" I asked.

"He never brought it up again."

"But you forgave him?"

"I forgave him."

As tears glistened in Joel's eyes, I realized he had managed to break the cycle of anger that his grandfather passed down to his dad.

Joel has two adult sons, neither of whom seemed to have an issue managing their anger. Since I was in the middle of writing this book on anger at the time, I asked Joel if we could talk further and if I could talk to his sons as well. When I explained why, he said he would set it up. Before he left, I gave him a copy of the chapters I'd already written. What I would discover when the four of us met a few weeks later provided a blueprint for how a father can break the cycle of generational anger.

BREAKING THE CYCLE OF ANGER

Joel and his two sons, Kip, twenty-eight, and Kerry, thirty-one, joined me at my home on a Saturday morning. It was early October and, knowing it might be the last day of the season dry enough to offer a view from my deck, I set our breakfast table there. I relish cooking—pun intended—so I prepared scrambled eggs spiced with coriander, chopped onions, red chili pepper, chopped jalapeños, and Swiss cheese. I also served fried potatoes, fresh fruit, bacon, and coffee from beans I had roasted the day before. This was a man's meal, and I knew they'd be impressed.

"I don't like cheese," Kip said, when I handed him his plate.

"And I don't like jalapeños," Kerry said.

"But together they're excellent!" Kip said.

"Right," Kerry said as he savored eggs unlike anything he had ever tasted before.

"You put up with this bantering all the time?" I asked Joel.

"Pretty much," he said.

"Bill, you've got to be kidding," Kip said. "We got our sarcasm from Dad. We've had to put up with him all of our lives. At least he's only had to endure us part of his."

I knew I'd have to be quick to keep up with these two guys. Fortunately, they were hungry and dug right into their breakfasts. We ate in silence for a few minutes, watching a turkey vulture swoop through the air before finally landing on one of the old growth fir trees in the ravine behind my house.

As I refilled their coffee mugs, I asked Kip and Kerry about their work. Kip had recently finished his medical residency and joined a clinic in Portland. Like his dad, he had a wiry frame and black hair, which he cut short. His twinkling eyes indicated he always had something funny to say even if he didn't say it—which proved to be seldom. Kerry stood nearly six feet tall and was built like a Mack truck. He had cannons for arms and tree trunks for legs. His black hair hung down to his collar. Kerry designed shoes for Nike, and his relaxed nature and casual clothes made him look like a West Coast artist.

Once they had finished eating, I asked Kerry and Kip if they knew why we were meeting.

"Dad told us," Kip said. "And I want you to know that Kerry and I are angry we had to get up so early on a Saturday morning to meet with you."

"I'm glad you're angry," I said. "I'll get to see how you process it."

The three nodded and laughed. "On a more serious note," I said. "You're both aware that your grandfather accused your dad of stealing his classic car?"

"Didn't he steal it?" Kip said.

"Yeah, I thought Dad stole it," Kerry interjected with a smile. "That's what Gramps said."

"I used to see Dad sneaking money out of Mom's purse," Kip said. "And once when I was a kid, I saw him creep into my room and take some of my candy."

Joel shook his head from side to side as his sons teased him. "Okay, guys, we need to shift gears. Let's put the joking aside."

"Seriously," Kerry said, "we knew Gramps was angry. But he wasn't just angry with Dad. And, yes, he told us Dad stole his car. But that's crazy."

"Now if he had accused Dad of taking candy from his room," Kip said jokingly, "we might have believed him."

Ignoring Kip's remark, I asked if Joel had gotten angry about his dad's accusation.

"Not really," Kip said. "He seemed hurt, but not angry."

"What did he say?"

"He said he wasn't sure why Gramps would say something so mean but thought it had to do with his own childhood," Kip said.

DON'T SPREAD BITTERNESS

"How about when other people disrespected or hurt your dad? How would he handle that?" I asked.

"I don't know," Kerry said. "He seldom discussed it with us."

That answer surprised me. "Joel, why didn't you?"

"Sue and I made a decision before the boys were born not to talk a lot about the wrongs we suffered in front of them."

"What do you mean?"

"I mean we would mention it if something hurtful happened but would only share the basic story in a way that didn't infect them with bitterness."

> **"We based our decision on Hebrews 12:15, which says, 'See to it that no one misses the grace of God and that no bitter root grows up to cause trouble and defile many.'"** (NIV)

"I think that passage describes the heart as a garden," Joel said. "Seeds, in the form of words, enter it through the ear canal. Once in the garden, the seeds germinate. Roots grow. A plant grows. It produces a flower that blossoms and then makes seeds. The seeds blow out of the heart through a person's mouth in the form of words that enter other gardens. In that way bitterness spreads from one person to another."

"Cool description," I said.

"I prefer the alternative to bitterness," Joel said.

"What's that?" I asked.

"When we spread bitterness we've missed out on the grace of God. The alternative is to allow God's grace to weed bitterness from our hearts."

"How would you do that?"

"Funny you should ask," Joel said. "You know the chapter in your new book on forgiveness? I'd say it captures how I tried to deal with my feelings when I was wronged. God's grace enables me to forgive as I've been forgiven. It enables me to review, not how someone has wronged me, but what good the person may have done. It enables me to pray for that person and see his or her point of view. That's what I learned to do with my dad, and it's what Sue and I have tried to do through the years when we've been hurt. And I believe it's how we've protected the boys from expressing their anger inappropriately when they've been wronged."

TALK THROUGH ANGER

"How about when you got mad at one of the boys? What did you do then?"

"I can answer that," Kip said. "Most of the time he would let us know he was angry and why."

"Did he ever yell or call you degrading names?"

"Of course he yelled, but not very often. And I'm sure he never called either of us a degrading name."

"When you were young, did he ever discipline you when angry?"

"If he was mad, he would send us to our room. Later, when he had cooled down, he would talk with us. I don't mean that he wasn't intense at times, but he never lashed out at us or said or did something to hurt us when he was angry."

"How about when the two of you argued with each other? What would he do then?"

"He insisted we sit down and talk through whatever issue triggered the argument," Kerry said. "Usually one of us had done something to start the fight and had to admit the wrong and ask for forgiveness. And since we were usually both guilty, we both had to own our part in the argument."

"Actually, Kerry usually started it," Kip said. "He became skilled at apologizing."

I ignored Kip's sarcasm and asked, "How has that helped you as adults?"

"When I have a problem with my wife or someone else, I talk to them instead of just stewing in my anger," Kerry said.

"I don't have a wife," Kip said. "But I think that since Dad wouldn't let us allow our anger to fester, it protected us from bitterness. If we bad-mouthed someone who had wronged us at school or in sports, he would immediately talk to us about it. He helped us see the other person's point of view. He would urge us to pray for them."

"So Joel, instead of passing your anger to your kids, you processed it with God and taught them to do the same?"

"I tried," Joel said.

BLESS YOUR CHILDREN

"I think you did something else," I said. "I believe you blessed your sons by giving them approval, security, and value. In the Old Testament times, a father used a blessing to transfer a good thing from one person to another. When Isaac blessed Jacob, he imparted the promise of bountiful crops, many servants, and leadership in the family.[1] In the New Testament, Jesus took children in his arms and blessed them.[2]"

I explained that while doing research for my book, I had surveyed thousands of men across the United States to learn more about their anger. One survey was designed to determine the relationship between a man's anger and whether or not he believed his father had blessed him.

"Here are the results of that survey," I said as I handed Joel a sheet of paper containing the following information:

54 percent of the surveyed men said their fathers had blessed them.

46 percent said they had not.

Of those who had not been blessed by their fathers, 63 percent said a family member or friend had told them they have an anger problem.

37 percent of those who had been blessed by their dads had gotten the same feedback.

Interestingly, those men who had not received a blessing from their dads felt they received less respect from their wives and their children than those men who had been blessed.

> **The survey results indicate that if a man wants to break the generational chain of anger, it's crucial for him to bless his son(s).**

As Joel returned the survey results to me, I said, "It seems clear to me, Joel, that you must have blessed your sons. How did you do that?"

Give verbal affirmation

"Before Dad answers, I'd like to tell you what he did from my point of view," Kerry interjected.

"Go ahead," I said.

"Dad always spoke words of encouragement. It's not that he didn't correct me; he did. But he offered more words of support than criticism."

"He always communicated his support," Kip said. "Even when I would do something stupid—like the time I put the car in reverse instead of drive and backed into a car that was parked behind me. He just shook his head and said the same thing happened to him once."

A shadow crossed Joel's face and he said, "My dad would often bless me with words of encouragement. And then he would steal the blessing away," Joel said. "Like with the T-Bird. One day he gave it to me, and the next month he accused me of stealing it. I didn't want to do that with Kerry and Kip."

Give physical affection

"My dad never hugged me or wrestled with me," Joel said. "He didn't think physical affection between men was appropriate . . . even between a father and son. When he lived with us, I would hug him and kiss him on the cheek. I still remember the smell of Old Spice on his neck. But I can remember only one time when he ever put his arms around me."

Kerry and Kip looked at each other and smiled. "Dad used to wrestle with us all the time," Kip said.

"But he quit when he knew we could take him down," Kerry said.

"You're right about that," Joel interjected, laughing.

"Even though we're now men, he never greets us or says good-bye without a hug and a kiss on the cheek," Kip said.

52 percent of surveyed men felt their dads showed them excellent or good respect.

22 percent felt it was terrible or poor.

"It goes back to the example of Jesus," Joel said. "He took the children in his arms and blessed them."

Offer visionary prayers

"There's something else Dad did when we were growing up," Kerry said. "He would put us in bed at night and pray for us. And his prayers always focused on how he believed God would use us in the future. Even as a kid I was artistic, and he prayed that my creative genius—he actually used the word *genius*— would be used by God to help people. And now I design shoes that people wear all over the world."

"And I always loved science," Kip said. "At night Dad would pray that God would use this interest to expand his Kingdom."

> "I don't know how he knew, but
> Dad sensed how God had wired us
> and he consistently expressed his belief
> that we were special and would
> be greatly used by God."

"You talk about a man's respect bank in your book," Joel added. "I think I succeeded in keeping Kerry's and Kip's respect banks full. Even when we had problems, I let them know I respected them."

Provide a biblical life view

"What about that project we each did with Dad when we reached our twelfth birthday?" Kerry said, looking at his brother. "That was important."

"And the reward was fun," Kip said.

"They're talking about the Passage," Joel said.

"What's that?" I asked.

"When each boy turned twelve, I had him work through a study from the book of Proverbs. The study focused on important subjects like money, sex, alcohol, laziness, wisdom, and foolishness. Each subject included verses from Proverbs. I gave each boy one month to study a subject and summarize what Proverbs taught about it.

"Next each was expected to write out a timeless principle based on his summary and explain how he would put it into practice. Finally, in every area of study he was to set personal life goals that supported the vision statement he had developed. At the end of the month he would share what he had written with the rest of the family."

"And Dad rewarded us with a trip when we'd finished," Kip said.

"He and I biked the Oregon coast," Kerry said. "It was a blast."

"He took me skiing at Mt. Bachelor for a week," Kip said. "Just the two of us."

A PICTURE OF LOVE

After the men had left, I returned to the deck and watched four vultures soar on the thermals looking for something dead to eat. And I contemplated how our flesh, like those vultures, is looking for an opportunity to feed on the wrongs we've suffered so that it can nourish bitterness and anger. Clearly Joel had helped teach his sons how to deny their flesh and nurture the new man in them so that they could manage their anger. His love had broken the generational cycle of anger.

A few days later Joel returned with something he wanted to show me. He handed me a photograph of a boy and his dad, both wearing baseball caps and smiling broadly. The boy held a trophy. The man knelt behind the boy, hugging him tightly with both arms.

"After Dad's death," Joel said, "I was cleaning out the T-Bird when I found this black-and-white photograph in the glove compartment. It was a picture of the only time I remember Dad hugging me.

"You asked me how I forgave him," he continued. "God used this picture. Inside my dad's most precious possession was his favorite picture. At least . . . I like to think it must have been. When I saw the picture I broke down and cried. In that moment God replaced my anger with the childlike love I once had for my dad. In spite of all he had done wrong as a dad, I had plenty of good memories to hold on to. And I decided I would rather live with those memories.

"I know when I die, my sons won't have to find a picture to remind them of my love. Every day . . . when I can . . . I tell them how much better my life is because of them."

TRUTHS TO LIVE BY
- I can break the generational cycle of anger.
- When I laugh with my kids, I give them joy instead of anger.
- I protect my children from anger by not spreading bitterness.
- I develop healthy children by teaching them to talk through anger.
- I bless my children by giving them positive verbal affirmation.
- I bless my children by giving them physical affection.
- I bless my children with visionary prayers.
- I bless my children by helping them develop a biblical life view.

STRENGTHEN THE GOOD MAN
Look after each other so that none of you fails to receive the grace of God. Watch out that no poisonous root of bitterness grows up to trouble you, corrupting many. (HEBREWS 12:15)
He said to them, "Let the children come to me. Don't stop them! For the Kingdom of God belongs to those who are like these children. I tell you the truth, anyone who doesn't receive the

Kingdom of God like a child will never enter it." Then he took the children in his arms and placed his hands on their heads and blessed them. (MARK 10:14-16)

DISCUSSION QUESTIONS

1. Read Mark 10:13-16 and talk about how Jesus blessed the children.

2. Did you receive your father's blessing? How has that affected you?

3. Why is it important to break the generational cycle of anger?

4. Why is it important for a father not to pass on bitterness to his kids? How can he protect his children from bitterness? Even if you don't have children, what can you do to not pass on bitterness to others?

5. What are the four ways Joel blessed his sons? Which most impressed you? How do you feel you're doing in each of those four areas? If you're single, how can you bless your family and friends?

6. How does your flesh try to use bitterness to nurture anger? How can you allow the new and good man in you to process bitterness in a healthy way?

7. What's the most important lesson you've learned from this book?

CHAPTER 9

THE WOMAN WITH A WHITE MARBLE IN HER HAND

Responding

WEARING BLACK SLACKS and a black blouse, Chris entered my office and sat in the leather chair closest to the fireplace. She brushed back her shoulder-length black hair and smiled. "I can't believe how much better Jim's doing," she said.

It had been a week since our intensive counseling sessions in which Jim embraced the truth about how pride was fueling his anger. (His story is found in chapter 6—and I'm telling Chris's side of the story, not because every woman has the same struggles she has with her husband's anger, but because many women would benefit from what she learned.)[1]

"I'm glad to hear that," I said. "What's changed?"

"I think the biggest difference is in the way he talks to me. He doesn't talk down to me like he used to. Just last night when he got home he saw an overdue notice from our doctor sitting on the kitchen table. Rather than lecturing me on how irresponsible I am, he calmly asked me about it and listened as I reminded him that our insurance company told us not to pay that bill until they'd finished processing it."

"That's good to hear. Hopefully, he'll keep growing."

"I think he will," Chris said. "Last week was the first time he's admitted he's got an anger issue. But I wanted to talk with you one-on-one because you mentioned there might be some ways I could encourage Jim as he seeks to control his anger."

"Thanks for following through, Chris. While Jim needs to learn to change the way he reacts when he's angry, I think you can interact with him in some ways that won't feed his anger or trigger one of his lectures."

"I'm all for that," Chris said.

"Let's start by looking at how you've interacted with Jim in the past. When he was angry, is it possible you went a bit too far to try to figure out the root of his problem so that you could help him?"

"What do you mean?"

"Jim told me you thought he had a sexual addiction, and in order to find out, you researched the subject and checked his Web browser history. He said when he denied it you told his pastor."

"That's because he *had* gone to a porn site."

"And how did you find that out?"

"He told me," she said. "He said it was an accident, but I didn't believe him."

"Do you believe him now?"

"I guess I do," she said.

I paused a moment so she could contemplate her admission. "Chris, how did he respond to your attempts to get him to admit he had a problem that he denied having?"

"He got defensive and angry."

*39 percent of surveyed women said their
husbands get angry more than once a week.*

13 percent said they get angry every day.

"After that situation Jim told me you read a book on marriage counseling that convinced you he was a misogynist. You believed he hated women."

"Yeah, I guess that seems a bit weird," she said. "But he was so angry with me all the time I thought it was a possibility."

"And how did he respond when you told him he was a misogynist?"

"At first he thought it was funny. When he realized I was serious, he began to gather evidence to prove I was wrong. You know how he can be. The more he argued with me, the more I disagreed and the angrier we got."

"Do you still think he hates women?"

"You're trying to show me a pattern, aren't you?"

"Do you see one?" I asked.

Chris gazed at me for several seconds and nodded her head. "This is hard to admit," she said. "Jim always said I was trying to change him. If I acknowledge a pattern like this, I'll be admitting he was right. In the past he would have used that against me."

A FAMILY ALBUM

"But it's just the two of us talking, Chris. Jim isn't here. I'm trying to help you get at the truth so you and Jim can build a stronger marriage. Jim's got his work cut out for him, but you

might consider changing your own pattern of thinking and acting, which only feeds his anger."

*13 percent of surveyed women said
they often try to fix their husbands.*

*42 percent said they sometimes
try to fix them.*

31 percent said they seldom try to fix them.

I then introduced Chris to the concept of codependence.
The word *codependent* isn't in vogue today as it was in the past,
but it's still the best word I know to describe certain kinds of
people and their behavior. I suspect at one time or another it
describes us all. My favorite definition is the one coined by
Melody Beattie. She says that codependents are people who
let another person's behavior affect them and who are obsessed
with controlling that person's behavior.[2] Codependents are so
focused on rescuing others that they ignore what's happening
inside themselves.

As children we all learn unwritten rules for relating to other
people. Children raised in dysfunctional families—families that
don't function in a healthy way—learn to react to the primary
stressor in the family. This could be a parent's alcohol or work
addiction, physical or verbal abuse, emotional control, religious
rigidity, or sexual abuse.[3]

Each child individually adapts to the stress caused by a parent's dysfunction in an attempt to control it and bring balance
to the family. Over time, each one assumes a codependent role
in the family.

For instance, one child may assume the role of the *family hero* who is out to save the family name. He is usually driven to excel in everything he does. Another child will take on the role of the *comedian* to provide comic relief for the family and divert attention from the real issues. Still another child may become the *family scapegoat*. She detracts attention from the problem with inappropriate and sometimes antisocial behavior. Other children in dysfunctional families may assume the role of the *family helper*, the *surrogate spouse,* or the *parent's parent.*

When the children of dysfunctional families grow up, they continue playing their roles even though they are no longer connected to the original sources of their stress. Their roles seem normal to them since they grew up with them. But even though these roles were helpful at one time, they eventually become destructive.[4]

As Chris and I talked, it became clear she had assumed the role of *family helper* because her parents' personal problems kept them from giving their children the attention they needed. She often disciplined her younger brother and sister, helped with their homework, and monitored their progress at school. She even did the laundry for them and ironed their clothes.

"I love my parents, Bill," she said. "And when I look back I have fond childhood memories. But it never occurred to me that I'm treating Jim like I did my brother and sister. No wonder it makes him mad."

WHO'S THE VICTIM?

"Anger is often the way someone responds when a well-intending family member or friend tries to fix them," I said. "A codependent person acts out of a desire to rescue someone. When the person being rescued doesn't respond in the desired way, the codependent gets mad and punishes the person. Finally, the codependent feels used and ends up being punished by the person the codependent tried to rescue. Ultimately, the person trying to rescue the other person ends up as the victim."[5]

18 percent of surveyed women said their husbands often get angry when they try to help them deal with an issue in their lives.

38 percent of the women said it sometimes makes them angry.

23 percent said it seldom makes them angry.

"That's exactly what happened to me!" Chris exclaimed. "I tried to help Jim with his porn problem, which I now know he didn't have. When he didn't respond like I wanted I got mad and punished him by calling the pastor. That made him even madder, and he punished me. I ended up as the victim. That has happened over and over again."

MEN NEED RESPECT

"Your obsession with fixing Jim triggered his anger because he felt disrespected by you," I said. "While women need to feel loved by their husbands, men need to feel respected by their wives. When you focus on how you think Jim needs to change and try to facilitate that change, he feels you don't respect his ability to work through his personal issues himself."

"But I'm not sure he can," she said.

"Maybe he can't, but you need to respect him enough to step back and let him try. If he wants your help, he'll ask for it."

"And if he doesn't?"

"Whether or not he asks for your help, you need to trust God to change him. Remember, Paul said in Philippians 1:6, 'And I am certain that God, who began the good work within you, will continue his work until it is finally finished on the day when Christ Jesus returns.'"

> **"By stepping aside you'll actually be allowing God to work in Jim. Your efforts may be fueling Jim's anger, which short-circuits God's work in his life."**

As the session concluded, I wrote Philippians 1:6 on an index card and handed it to Chris. I asked her to keep it with her and read it every time she felt compelled to change Jim or give him unrequested help.

After Chris left, I recalled an ongoing conflict my wife and I had during the first year of our marriage. Cindy repeatedly tried to get me to stop watching so much TV. She would kindly plead with me to turn it off. She would demand I turn it off. She would turn it off while I was watching a football game. She would quote from Proverbs about the dangers of laziness. The more she tried to change me, the angrier I got . . . and the more TV I watched.

One day Cindy stopped talking about my viewing habits.

She even acted like my watching TV had no effect on her. But behind the scenes she was praying that God would change me.

Several months after her moratorium started I heard a business leader, Arthur S. DeMoss, give a speech in which he said he had no TVs in his home. He listed the benefits he and his family had reaped because they had no TVs. He stressed that it wasn't a dictatorial decision he made, but one the family voted on every year. When I got home, I called a friend and gave him our television. Cindy and I actually survived for seven years without a television, and I'm sure it helped our relationship. When we finally got another one, it was a mutual decision.

That experience served as a life-changing and marriage-enhancing experience for Cindy. She discovered that God would work better and quicker in my life if she would get out of the way and let him change me. It's a lesson that's been validated numerous times over the course of our marriage. In fact, I can think of two specific changes that occurred in my life last year that were a result of her prayers—changes she initially tried to pressure me into making before backing off and bringing the matters to God.

Men need the respect of their wives. And when they don't get it, their immediate reaction is often anger. Anger that leads to abusive behavior should *never* be tolerated. However, after working with Chris and Jim, I knew both spouses were committed to loving and respecting each other.

FINDING A WAY OUT

Often when someone I counsel has a breakthrough in understanding like Chris had, he or she expects change to happen quickly. When I met with Chris again, she admitted that keeping herself from attempting to control Jim was much harder than she had expected, in part because she was disappointed when he would not change in the way she wanted.

13 percent of surveyed women said they are often disappointed with their husbands.

43 percent said they are sometimes disappointed with them.

30 percent said they are seldom disappointed with them.

We talked about how Chris's childhood role of helper made her seek a marriage partner to whom she could relate in the same way. As illogical as it sounds, Chris felt responsible for Jim's shortcomings, just as she had assumed responsibility for the shortcomings of her brother and sister. The guilt she felt about his shortcomings actually drove her harder to fix him. When he still didn't change, Chris often felt anger.

Once she admitted this pattern, we discussed how she could help bring about change in her marriage by working on herself. As you consider how to respond to an angry husband or loved one, these principles may help you too.

PRAYERFULLY REFLECT ON YOUR PAST

"Can you see how your role as the helper in your family growing up programmed you to search out such a relationship?"

"You mean I actually wanted to marry someone I thought needed my help?"

"What do you think?"

"It makes sense," she said. "I've been trying to fix Jim for much of our marriage."

"And do you ever feel responsible for Jim's shortcomings?"

"Not really," she said. And then she paused a moment. "Maybe a little."

"That guilt may drive you to try harder to fix him to relieve your guilt. And when he resists your efforts and doesn't change, it may fuel your anger. Such anger is unhealthy because it results from an unmet expectation.

"When that kind of anger is suppressed, it can cause ongoing feelings of rage that can occasionally explode."

"Like the time I lost my temper and threw something at Jim?"

18 percent of surveyed women said
when they and their husbands argue they
usually argue and then forget about it.

20 percent said they argue and then
withdraw for a few days or weeks.

9 percent said they argue and
then withhold affection.

39 percent said they argue
and then work through it.

"That's a good example," I said. "Of course, not everyone has angry outbursts. Some women use sarcasm or withhold affection to express anger."

"This is helpful, Bill, but I want to know how I can get past it all."

"Chris, it's important for you to know that neither you nor Jim will get past all of this as though you've left a building. It's going to take time and you'll occasionally fall into the old destructive patterns. It's going to require some work.

"I want to encourage you to take some time alone and prayerfully reflect on the role you had in your family while growing up. Look at your present relationships and see how you still function in that role. Take a notepad and write down your thoughts.

"Don't look for someone else to blame for your present problems. Instead, try to understand why you are the way you are so you can more easily change."

"I've been doing that since our last meeting," she said. "I've even jotted down some thoughts in my journal."

LET GO

"Keep it up," I said. "As you better understand why you sometimes try to change Jim, it will be easier for you to overcome your urge to hold on and try to control him. While holding on seems like the safe thing to do, it isn't.

"Have you ever gotten better because someone forced you to change?" I asked.

Chris laughed and shook her head. "No way!"

"Like the father of the Prodigal Son, you need to let Jim go. You need to trust that God will work in his life."

"But what if he's doing something that's wrong? Should I not say anything?"

"Letting go doesn't mean you approve of wrong behavior. Nor does it mean you never confront it. And it certainly doesn't mean you don't care. Instead, you need to stop allowing yourself to be obsessed with rescuing Jim by controlling his life and fixing his flaws. He interprets that as disrespect, and it feeds his anger."

Chris committed to reflect on her past and come back the next week with insights she had jotted down in her journal. She also agreed to consciously choose to thank God for something about Jim every time she was tempted to focus on his flaws. And finally, she said she would make a conscious effort to let go of Jim and trust God to change him.

FIND THE NEW YOU

When we met the following week I talked with Chris about how showing Jim respect by not trying to change him involved more than just breaking away from the role she learned as a child. We talked about how her identity should not rest in her role as Jim's helper. While fixing Jim, or attempting to do so, might make her feel secure, needed, and even righteous, it gave her a flawed sense of identity. Her true identity rests in the fact that she's a new and good woman in Christ. After we had talked about some of the identity issues I've discussed in this book, I gave her some coaching tips.

HOW TO RESPOND TO AN ANGRY MAN

"Before the three of us met, how would you normally respond when Jim would get angry?" I asked Chris.

"Since he would often talk in a robotic tone and overwhelm me with facts proving I was wrong, I would defend myself."

"And would you convince him he was wrong?"

"Never," she said. "He would just argue more forcefully. And then I'd get mad."

"That was a painful cycle for both of you."
"Yes, it was."

> 17 percent of surveyed women said
> they often have a plan for dealing
> with their husbands' anger.
>
> 32 percent said they sometimes have a plan.
>
> 28 percent said they seldom have a plan.
>
> 18 percent said they never have a plan.

"Since trying to defend yourself didn't work, I'd like to offer you some ideas that will lead to a better result."

"I'm all ears," Chris said.[6]

LISTEN AND DEFLECT

The Bible provides some great insights into how to respond to an angry person.

> *A gentle answer deflects anger, but harsh words make tempers flare.* (PROVERBS 15:1)

> *This you know, my beloved brethren. But everyone must be quick to hear, slow to speak and slow to anger; for the anger of man does not achieve the righteousness of God.* (JAMES 1:19-20, NASB)

After Chris read these two passages, she said, "It's pretty clear I need to respond to Jim's anger by gently listening to him while bridling my own anger."

"Let's consider an example," I said. "Remember the time you and Jim argued about who had failed to fill up his car with gas? Suppose instead of defending yourself, you had listened to his expression of anger and simply deflected it without allowing your own emotions to get stirred up?"

"How would I have done that?" she asked.

"As you allowed him to talk, you'd imagine yourself in a protective bubble, which would allow you to let him vent his anger without any of his emotion getting to you.

"You'd visualize all his words and feelings deflecting off this bubble and falling harmlessly to the floor. That would allow you to listen without his anger triggering your anger. So if he were to say, 'Chris, why did you drive my car and bring it home without gas?' you would hear his words without feeling a need to defend yourself."

LISTEN AND EMPATHIZE

"Once Jim had expressed his feelings, the next step would be for you to respond in a way that allowed him to tell his story again so you could express empathy. You might have gently said, 'Jim, tell me again exactly what happened and why you're angry.'"

"He would have still been mad," she said.

"I think you're right."

> **"But at that point in the conversation
> you're trying to understand his anger
> so you can help him process it, not
> so you can argue with him."**

"After he told you again why he was angry you might have expressed empathy by saying, 'Jim, no wonder you're mad. I would be mad, too, if I had asked you to put gas in my car and instead you took it to the store and returned it empty.'

"Hopefully, by then his anger would have subsided enough that he would be willing to listen to what you have to say."

GENTLY EXPLAIN

"Instead of defending yourself, you would then explain what happened. You might have calmly said, 'Jim, may I please tell you what happened? I took my car to the store. If your car was driven, it must have been one of the kids. Let's talk with them and see if they drove it or not. If they did drive it, we need to remind them of the importance of not bringing a car home without gas.'"

"And what if he was still mad?"

QUIETLY STEP AWAY

"If he was still mad, then you would need to tell him you understand his anger but think it would better to discuss it with him after you'd talked with the kids. Once you talked with them, you could tell Jim they had driven the car."

Chris nodded.

Then I asked her, "But suppose you had driven his car? What would you have done then?"

"But I didn't."

"I know, Chris. I'm presenting a hypothetical situation. If you had driven his car, what would you have done then?"

WHEN APPROPRIATE SEEK FORGIVENESS

"If I had driven his car, I would have apologized and asked him to forgive me."

"That's a good idea. But it would be wise to apologize *after* taking the first two steps. That would allow him to express his anger so that when you explained what happened he would feel you understood the wrong he endured."

"That makes sense," Chris said. "I'll start working on these tips this week and let you know how it goes."

THE FOLLOW-UP

When Chris and I met in my office after she had been practicing these techniques for a few weeks, the first thing I noticed was a gleam in her eyes.

"You look like you're hiding a secret," I said.

"I figured out something that has made a big difference in how I respond to Jim's anger."

"I thought he was controlling his anger," I said.

"Oh, he's doing much better," Chris said. "But my *secret* has helped."

"Tell me about it."

Chris slipped her right hand into her right jeans pocket. When she pulled it out she held an object in her clenched fist. "It's here, in my hand."

"What is it?"

Chris slowly opened her hand, revealing a white marble. "It took me a while to find a white one, but I succeeded," she said, smiling. "It's Jim."

"Hmmm. He looks much smaller. And more spherical," I said.

Ignoring my attempt at humor, she said, "I wanted a white marble because the white reminds me that in Christ Jim's a new man—a good man. It reminds me that Christ is at work in his life."

"That's cool," I said.

"Whenever I find myself thinking about fixing him, changing him, or reacting to his anger, I grab the marble and then release it. It's a reminder that I've got to let go of Jim and let God change him. It reminds me to release my anger so that I don't react in a way that makes things worse."

"Jim's a lucky man," I said.

"Lucky? Come on, Bill, you know it's got nothing to do with luck."

"What do you mean?"

"I mean I'm a gift from God."

She was right, of course. As is every wife.

TRUTHS TO LIVE BY

- Men need the respect of their spouses and loved ones.
- I can show my husband respect by trusting God to change him.
- For the sake of myself and my children, I will never excuse abusive behavior from my husband.
- When my husband is angry, I will listen and deflect.
- I will respond to my husband's anger by listening and empathizing.

- I will respond to my husband's anger by gently explaining what happened from my perspective.
- I will respond to my husband's anger by quietly stepping away.
- When appropriate, I will ask for forgiveness.

STRENGTHEN THE GOOD WOMAN

And I am certain that God, who began the good work within you, will continue his work until it is finally finished on the day when Christ Jesus returns. (PHILIPPIANS 1:6)

A gentle answer deflects anger, but harsh words make tempers flare. (PROVERBS 15:1)

This you know, my beloved brethren. But everyone must be quick to hear, slow to speak and slow to anger; for the anger of man does not achieve the righteousness of God. (JAMES 1:19-20, NASB)

THE NEW YOU
EVERY MAN HAS A STORY

"FIGHT AND YOU may die. Run and you'll live . . . at least a while. And dying in your beds, many years from now, would you be willing to trade *all* the days, from this day to that, for one chance, just one chance, to come back here and tell our enemies that they may take our lives, but they'll never take . . . *our freedom!*"

Those words were uttered by William Wallace—actually it was Mel Gibson playing the role of the fourteenth-century Scottish rebel—prior to a strategic battle. As his army of ragtag amateurs looked across the valley at the armed-to-their-teeth British troops, the men questioned the wisdom of fighting a battle they seemed certain to lose. The Scots looked as doomed to defeat as a rowboat shooting it out with a battleship. And Wallace's uprising against the English ruler set on grabbing Scotland's crown seemed just as hopeless.

But in the movie *Braveheart*, the words of Wallace rallied his army and they fought and won and lived to fight another day.

As you can tell from this book, I like stories. I like them because each man's life is a story. And in every story, you've got a hero, a villain, a conflict, and a point of despair when failure seems certain. And then an insight, a cause, a love for God, a woman, or a family will enable the hero to overcome a personal weakness and insurmountable odds to accomplish the impossible. This will lead to the resolution of the crisis and a new, positive direction for the hero and those he loves. In every good story, the hero changes. He's a different and hopefully a better man on the final page.

Those are the kinds of stories I like. In a tragedy, the hero comes to an unhappy or disastrous ending brought on by "moral weakness, psychological maladjustment, or social pressures."[1] *Braveheart* wasn't a tragedy, even though William Wallace died. That's because he died a martyr. His is the story of a pacifist turned warrior turned hero. His dying cry, as his body was stretched on the rack, was "Freedom!"

Some real-life stories are heartbreaking tragedies, like the story of Jeff. He and I had only met a few times when I realized Jeff had suffered some terrible wrongs at the hands of a brother and a former friend. Rather than working through his anger and forgiving those who had wronged him, he nursed his bitterness until it grew into hatred that morphed into rage. Rather than processing his anger in a healthy way, he chose to medicate it with alcohol. Eventually he became a full-blown alcoholic. While he made a lot of money selling stuff—I don't remember what he sold, just that he sold a lot of it—he refused to take the painful steps necessary to deal with his anger and stop drinking. One day he told me he had blacked out and couldn't remember where he had parked his car. He didn't even remember how he got home.

I will never forget that meeting. I pleaded with him to

embrace the grace of God and consider forgiving his enemies. He refused even to consider my suggestion. I asked him to get into an alcohol treatment program. He said he would do that someday. When he left that meeting I had a terrible feeling that I would never see him alive again.

A week later Jeff was sitting at his kitchen table drinking whiskey and cleaning a revolver while his twelve-year-old son watched. He pulled back the hammer and cocked the gun and then placed it to his right temple. He pulled the trigger, and his son listened as the gun clicked—the chamber was empty. Dangerously drunk, Jeff laughed at the relief on his terrified son's face. Assuming the gun was empty, he repeated the joke two more times. He didn't do it again because the third chamber contained a bullet that blew his brains out while his son watched.

Both William Wallace and Jeff died violent deaths. But Wallace died a hero, and he used his anger at a ruler's oppression of his people to galvanize an unlikely army to fight for Scotland's freedom. My friend refused to address his uncontrolled anger and died a drunk—his story left those who loved him sickened and sad.

Since you're still living, some of your story—and hopefully most of it—is yet to be written. Each of the stories I've told in this book is about a man who battled a villain—let's call it his flesh. The villain sought to control this man's destiny by turning his anger into a seething or explosive rage. Each man gained an insight that allowed the hero in him to realize he was a new and good man in Christ. That realization, along with other insights, enabled him to live progressively freer from the villain's power.

You alone will determine whether or not the leading

character of your story is a hero. You alone will decide if he will be an angry, spiteful man or a gracious, forgiving one. You will determine if he will allow his flesh or the new and good man to direct his life. You will decide, through a series of choices, what kind of story your wife, kids, grandkids, and friends will tell about you. In fact, they're already telling your story with the words they speak about you every day.

You can decide how your story will develop from here. While there are elements of your story over which you have no control, you alone must decide, by God's grace, how you will respond to circumstances, including the way you process and express your anger.

Maybe it would help if you took some time over the next week or so to write your story—the one in which you're the hero—and your personal battle with anger or other villains. It doesn't have to be long. You don't even need to write it for anyone else. Write it for yourself. (While I think writing would be helpful, since it's likely to lead to the most insights, you could simply think through your story if you'd prefer. Maybe you could tell it aloud to yourself and to God.)

As you plan the story, you'll want to think through the following questions. (Pages 157–160 are set aside for you to jot down your answers.) Describe the hero. What are his strengths, weaknesses, motivations, and character-shaping experiences? What drives his anger? Does it flow from a failure to recognize his new and true identity in Christ? Is he suffering from a respect deficit? Does he use anger to control others? Is he filled with pride? Does he need to forgive a wrong he's suffered? Does he need to bless his children in order to break the generational cycle of anger passed down by his dad?

As you develop your story, explain what triggers the hero's anger. All of this will set up the battle between the villain and hero. It's crucial for you to explain in detail the insight that will enable the hero to overcome the villain. What does he love so much that he's willing to make whatever sacrifice is necessary to achieve victory? And what is the source of power that enables him to live as a new and good man in Christ? Once you've answered these questions, consider reworking them into a few paragraphs that tell your story. If you'd like, you can write out your story in this book, beginning on page 161.

I hope you realize that your story isn't over and that the best part is yet to be lived. As you understand your new and true identity in Christ and allow the new and good man in you to process and express your anger, you will become a force to accomplish great good. And your life will tell others of the power of the One who has made you a good man.

NOTES ON YOUR STORY

Describe the hero (that would be you).

_____

_____

_____

What are his

Strengths?

_____

_____

_____

Weaknesses?

_____

_____

_____

Motivations?

_____

_____

_____

Character-shaping experiences?

_____

_____

_____

What drives his anger?

A failure to recognize his new and true identity in Christ?

_____

_____

_____

A respect deficit?

_____

_____

_____

A desire to control others?

_____

_____

_____

_____

Pride?

_____

_____

_____

Unforgiveness?

_____

_____

_____

Does he need to bless his children in order to break the generational cycle of anger passed down by his dad? If so, why?

_____

_____

_____

_____

What does he love so much that he's willing to make whatever sacrifice is necessary to achieve victory? What is the source of power that enables him to live as a new and good man in Christ?

YOUR STORY

_____

_____

_____

_____

_____

_____

_____

_____

_____

_____

_____

_____

_____

_____

MY STORY OF FAITH

Because the key to managing and expressing your anger flows from your new identity in Christ, it's crucial you actually embrace it. I mention this because while I occasionally attended church as a boy and young man, it wasn't until I was a college student that I actually understood what it meant to know Christ. I had heard about his death and resurrection, but my understanding was fuzzy, like an out-of-focus image in a camera viewfinder. Because of that I appreciated it when a friend took some time to show me from the Bible how I could know Christ. And for that reason I'd like to share with you what I learned back then that clarified my thinking and stimulated my faith.

For years I thought a Christian was someone whose good deeds outweighed his bad ones. I had an image of God in heaven holding a large scale. Every time I'd swear or get angry, he'd place a weight on the bad side of the scale. Whenever I'd do something good, he'd place a weight on the good side of the scale. I guess I thought he was like Santa Claus—except a lot more was at stake than what I'd get for Christmas.

As I reflected on how I thought, spoke, and acted, it became apparent that the scale was tipping in the wrong direction. That's no surprise since the Bible tells us, "For everyone has sinned; we all fall short of God's glorious standard" (Romans 3:23). And even the good deeds that I thought might win God's favor wouldn't tip the scale in my direction, according to the words of Isaiah 64:6: "We are all infected and impure with sin. When we display our righteous deeds, they are nothing but filthy rags."

Think about that for a moment . . . everything in my life that I viewed as righteous, everything I thought would tip the scale in my favor, God viewed as a pile of dirty rags. Why? Because he compared my goodness to his own.

Okay, so God's not like Santa Claus. He's not keeping a record of the naughty and nice things I do as a way of determining if he'll forgive my sins and give me eternal life. Once I gave up on that way of approaching God, I thought that maybe God would grade on the curve. The Bible clears up that misconception. It says, "For the person who keeps all of the laws except one is as guilty as a person who has broken all of God's laws" (James 2:10).

In other words, the laws of God are like a giant mirror. If one corner is cracked the mirror is called "broken." If I break even one of God's commandments—and I've broken most of them—I've broken his law as has the worst violator. The point isn't that all sins are equally bad, but that one sin makes me a violator of God's law and thus unworthy to enter his presence.

But it's worse than that. In Romans 6:23 Paul says, "For the wages of sin is death." The word *death* speaks of separation. Physical death refers to separation from the body; spiritual death speaks of separation from God. The consequence of my sin is eternal separation from the life of God. This bad news would be inescapable except that God made a way for my sins to be punished so I could be liberated from the penalty and enter his presence.

It's at this point that my understanding became blurred. And it's at this point that I want to be especially clear. Jesus did not die as a martyr. He did not die because he was in the wrong place at the wrong time—as I once thought. He died to make payment for your sins and mine and those of the rest of the world. Once I understood this, the image in the viewfinder appeared crisp and clear. I realized how God could accept me in spite of my sins.

The apostle Paul says it this way: "But God showed his great love for us by sending Christ to die for us while we were still sinners" (Romans 5:8). The key word in that sentence is the three-letter preposition *for*. It means "in the place of." Jesus died in our place.

When I was in college a friend explained it to me like this. Suppose you stole a car and while you were cruising around, a policeman spotted you. He turned on his flashing lights to pull you over, but instead of stopping you sped away. During the chase, you ran a red light, made an illegal turn, drove against oncoming traffic, and ran over a stop sign. After your arrest you stood before a judge who sentenced you to six months in jail or a $20,000 fine. Unable to pay the fine, you knew you'd be spending time behind bars. And then the unexpected happened: the judge paid your fine.

Upon leaving the courthouse if someone asked you, "Why are you free?" you would answer, "Because the judge paid my fine." That's what Jesus did for us on the cross. The apostle Paul puts it this way: "God made him who had no sin to be sin for us, so that in him we might become the righteousness of God" (2 Corinthians 5:21, NIV).

Because Jesus is fully God and fully man, he was able to take upon himself the sins of all mankind and pay in full the eternal debt we all deserved. But what he did is even better than that. The verse above says he did this "so that in him we might become the righteousness of God." It's as though the judge not only paid your fine but also deposited $100,000,000 into your account. Through his death and resurrection, Jesus paid our fine and deposited all of his righteousness into our spiritual account.

That's why we can enter God's presence. In Philippians 3:9 Paul says, "I no longer count on my own righteousness through obeying the law; rather, I become righteous through faith in Christ."

There is, however, a condition for all of this. We must accept Christ's payment on our behalf. In Ephesians 2:8-9 Paul writes, "God saved you by his grace when you believed. And you can't take credit for this; it is a gift from God. Salvation is not a reward for the good things we have done, so none of us can boast about it."

The words of Paul echo those of Jesus: "There is no judgment against anyone who believes in him. But anyone who does not believe in him has already been judged for not believing in God's one and only Son" (John 3:18).

The only thing God asks us to do to receive forgiveness and eternal life is to trust that through his death Jesus paid for our sins and through his resurrection he assures us of eternal life. The words *faith* or *believe* do not mean we simply give intellectual assent to the death and resurrection of Jesus. To place our faith in or to believe in Jesus is to trust in him. For instance, you may believe a plane will fly—that's intellectual assent. The moment you get on the plane and trust it to fly you to a destination, you've exercised faith. You may believe a doctor is qualified to operate on you—that's intellectual assent. The moment you climb on the gurney and let him perform surgery, you've exercised faith. You may believe Jesus lived and died as a historical character—that's intellectual assent. The moment you rely on him alone for forgiveness and eternal life, you've exercised faith.

It may be that when you first started reading this section, your understanding of what it means to be a Christian was as fuzzy as mine once was. If so, I hope what you've read has brought the image into sharp focus. I hope if you've never trusted Christ for forgiveness and eternal life, or if you're unsure if you have, you'll do so now. You could express your faith with a prayer like this, much as I did as a college student:

> Father, I thank you that you love me. I admit that I have sinned against you with my thoughts, words, and deeds. I now know that my sins have separated me from you and brought on me your deserved condemnation. But I believe that Jesus Christ, your Son, died on a cross in my place and rose from the dead. I believe his death paid in full the penalty for my sins. Right now I'm trusting in Jesus Christ alone for forgiveness and eternal life. Amen.

If you expressed your faith with a prayer like this, the Bible promises that all of your sins will be forgiven and God will give you eternal life (John 3:16; John 10:27-29). You'll also become a child of God (John 1:12), and you'll receive God's Spirit (Romans 8:15-17). Additionally, the message of this book will apply to you because you'll be a new man in Christ (2 Corinthians 5:17).

If you're still unsure about whether or not you know Christ, ask yourself the following question: If you got to heaven and God asked, "Why should I let you in?" what would you say?

If you would answer, "You should let me in because I've tried to be good," or, "I've been good," or, "I've been sincere *and* I believe in Christ," then you're not trusting Christ alone for forgiveness and eternal life. We've already seen that the Bible says none of us are good enough to earn God's favor.

The single answer that would give you assurance that your sins are forgiven and you have eternal life is, "I've trusted Christ alone for forgiveness and eternal life." This is what the Bible means when it says, "This is what God has testified: He has given us eternal life, and this life is in his Son. Whoever has the Son has life; whoever does not have God's Son does not have life" (1 John 5:11-12).

If you've trusted Christ and expressed your faith with that prayer, I want to be the first to welcome you into God's family. I'd love to know about your new faith and would appreciate if you'd let me know. I'd also encourage you to find a church where you can connect with other guys and grow spiritually.

Maybe you're still investigating the claims of Christ and the new life he offers. It could be you're not ready to trust him. If so, I hope this book provides you with insights that will stimulate your thinking and faith and help you better manage and express your anger.

PLEASE TAKE A BOW

THIS PAGE IS the stage I have cleared so that my friends who helped make this book a reality can take a bow. Of course, they would never do such a thing unless I pushed them out front—something I eagerly do. You may applaud as each one bows, or you may hold your applause until the end.

Many years ago while I was banging away on my Royal manual typewriter, my friend Rod Cooper asked me if I'd considered getting a computer. I said I hadn't. He then asked me to follow him to his office, where he displayed his magical box. I was converted on the spot and have Rod to thank for every word I type. But it was also Rod's influence in the publishing world that opened a critical door for me at a strategic time in my writing career. I told him I'd never forget, and I haven't. Every word you read in this book came through the door he opened.

It was John Van Diest who, as the publisher at another publishing house, released my first book—again, that was a long time ago. But in 2004 he introduced me to Tyndale House.

Thanks for believing in me and my words—you've been a great encouragement.

Jan Long Harris is the associate publisher at Tyndale who has coached me, encouraged me, and made me laugh. She has a quick mind and a great sense of humor. To know her is to smile.

Kim Miller is the editor who smoothed out the rough spots of the book so it would read better. And she did this without altering my voice. Thanks, Kim. She was ably assisted by Bonne Steffen, who oversaw the copyediting and proofreading.

Please give a round of applause to the unknown and unnamed team at Tyndale. A number of readers were given the unedited manuscript so they could read it and give it a thumbs-up or a thumbs-down—plus priceless feedback. I appreciate the time they took to read the book critically. Your insights helped make it better.

I'd also like to thank James C. Hassinger for his analysis of the survey data, and Dr. Rod Cooper—yes, the same Rod I noted above—and Rich Wold for their help with the development of the survey questions. I'm thankful to Mark Shirley for helping distribute the women's surveys to a wider Internet audience.

Of course, I give a standing ovation to the men and women whose stories are tweaked and then told in this book. Your willingness to let God work in your lives is a testament to his life-changing grace.

ABOUT THE AUTHOR

BILL PERKINS's wit, insight, and penetrating stories have made him a compelling voice in the Christian community. He has authored or collaborated on twenty books, including *When Good Men Are Tempted*, *Six Battles Every Man Must Win*, *6 Rules Every Man Must Break*, and *The Jesus Experiment*.

Bill has a passion for helping men discover their strength in God. He is the founder and CEO of Million Mighty Men and served as a senior pastor for twenty-four years. He holds degrees from the University of Texas and Dallas Theological Seminary.

With his talent for humor, candor, and tackling tough issues head-on, Bill is a sought-after speaker for both Christian and corporate groups. He has addressed men's groups across the world and conducted business and leadership seminars across the country for companies such as Alaska Airlines and McDonald's. He has led chapels for major league baseball teams, and appeared on nationally broadcast radio and television shows, including *The O'Reilly Factor*.

Bill and his wife, Cindy, live in West Linn, Oregon. They have three sons and two grandchildren.

For more information on Bill's ministries and to follow his blog, visit www.billperkins.com.

NOTES

CHAPTER 2: AN ALIEN EXPERIENCE

1. *American Heritage Dictionary of the English Language*, 4th ed., s.v. "alien."
2. Adapted from my book *When Good Men Are Tempted* (Grand Rapids, MI: Zondervan, 2007), 148–150.
3. Merriam-Webster Online Dictionary, http://www.merriam-webster.com.
4. Gary Chapman, *The Other Side of Love* (Chicago: Moody Press, 1999), 19.
5. Ibid., 20.
6. Ibid., 21.
7. Adapted from my book *6 Rules Every Man Must Break* (Carol Stream, IL: Tyndale, 2007), 86–87.
8. W. E. Vine, *Vine's Expository Dictionary of New Testament Words*, (McLean, VA: MacDonald Publishing Company, 1940), 57.
9. Adapted from *6 Rules Every Man Must Break*, 96–97.
10. Ibid., 93–95.

CHAPTER 3: THE MAN WITH A HOLE IN HIS FACE

1. I often use this illustration when counseling; I also included it in my book *When Good Men Are Tempted*, 158–160, from which this version is adapted.
2. Ephesians 2:3, NASB
3. I'm thankful to David Needham for the crab apple tree illustration. We did have crab apple trees at my home in Roswell, and they were bitter. See David Needham, *Birthright* (Sisters, OR: Multnomah Publishers, 1999), 82–84.

CHAPTER 4: THE MAN WHO WITHHELD SEX FROM HIS WIFE

1. To read about the leadership role God granted to Adam, see Genesis 1:26; 2:19-20.
2. Ephesians 5:33
3. I'm thankful to Willard F. Harley Jr. for the concept of the Love Bank. The Respect Bank grew out of this idea.

CHAPTER 5: THE MAN WHO YELLED AT HIS DAUGHTER

1. Mark 3:5

CHAPTER 6: THE MAN WHO WOULD BE GOD

1. Read about Satan's deception of Adam and Eve in Genesis 3.
2. This account is found in Genesis 4:1-9.
3. Proverbs 15:25
4. Matthew 12:34
5. James 1:19-20; Ephesians 4:26-27
6. By the way, after I wrote this chapter, I showed it to Jim, and he humbly gave his approval—with a few editorial suggestions.

CHAPTER 8: THE MAN ACCUSED OF STEALING FROM HIS DAD

1. Genesis 27:27-29
2. Mark 10:16

CHAPTER 9: THE WOMAN WITH A WHITE MARBLE IN HER HAND

1. If you're in an abusive situation, then the first and most important thing you can do is seek professional help. There are people who care and will provide you with assistance.
2. Melody Beattie, *Codependent No More* (San Francisco: Harper and Row, 1987), 31.
3. John Bradshaw, *Bradshaw on the Family* (Deerfield Beach, IL: Health Communications, 1988), 163–164.
4. Ibid., 165.
5. Claude M. Steiner, *Scripts People Live* (New York: Grove Press, 1974). These insights are drawn from the work of Dr. Stephen B. Karpman, who compares the roles a codependent plays to the three points of a triangle.
6. Gary Chapman, *The Other Side of Love* (Chicago: Moody Press, 1999), 167–177. I'm thankful for Chapman's insights in chapter 13 concerning what to do when you encounter an angry person.

AFTERTHOUGHTS: THE NEW YOU

1. *Webster's New World Dictionary*, s.v. "tragedy," www.yourdictionary.com.

ADDITIONAL RESOURCES

AFTER READING THE STORY of David's mighty men (found in 2 Samuel 22 and 23) a number of years ago, I sensed God calling me to encourage guys to become modern-day mighty men. I launched a ministry called Million Mighty Men with the belief that revival would come, one man and one day at a time. I also wrote the book *Six Battles Every Man Must Win* to show men how they can win the unseen war raging in their own hearts.

In this book, of course, I've focused on the battle so many men have with anger. If you'd like to regularly be challenged and encouraged in your fight to overcome destructive anger and other temptations, I invite you to go to www.billperkins. com and enter your name and e-mail address. You'll receive a weekly e-mail from me and become part of a movement of men who have decided to engage in this battle for our own hearts, homes, and the helpless.

If you want more information about our work with orphans or hosting a men's event at your church, ministry, or community, go to www.billperkins.com and click on the "host an event" tab.

|||

WHILE DOING RESEARCH for this book I found some excellent resources that I'd encourage you to read.

The Anger Trap (Jossey-Bass, 2004) by Dr. Les Carter is filled with excellent insights that will help you better understand yourself and your anger. Dr. Carter is a nationally recognized expert on the subject of anger, and if you read his book you'll know why. Almost every page of my copy is filled with underlined and starred statements.

Dr. Carter also authored, with Dr. Frank Minirth, *The Anger Workbook* (Thomas Nelson, 1992). This thirteen-step guide will help you identify and modify your destructive anger.

The Angry Man (W Pub Group, 1991) by Dr. David Stoop and Stephen Arterburn does an excellent job identifying some of the sources of male anger.

Beyond Anger . . . A Guide for Men (Marlowe & Company, 2000) by Thomas J. Harbin, Ph.D., provides an honest and tough look at male anger and how it can be managed. Because Dr. Harbin is a clinical psychologist in private practice specializing in the treatment of angry men, he includes a lot of clinical stories to illustrate his significant insights.

The Other Side of Love (Moody, 1999) by Dr. Gary Chapman is one of the best books I've read on anger. Dr. Chapman provides a biblical explanation of anger and how it can be used in a loving way.

Anger Reconciliation (SEL Publications, 2008) was written by James Offutt, who's spent fifteen years working with Teen Challenge in Syracuse, New York, and Orlando, Florida. During that time he has developed some excellent techniques geared to help men process and express their anger in a healthy way. This book is a quick read, but it's packed full of insights. You can learn more about the book and its author by going to http://www.angerispositive.com.

Finally, if you are the parent of teenagers, I encourage you to consider leading your kids through the Passage, which Joel describes on page 128. You can find more information at www.teenpassage.net.

Online Discussion Guide

TAKE YOUR TYNDALE READING
EXPERIENCE TO THE NEXT LEVEL

A FREE discussion guide for this book is available at bookclubhub.net, perfect for sparking conversations in your book group or for digging deeper into the text on your own.

www.bookclubhub.net

You'll also find free discussion guides for other Tyndale books, e-newsletters, e-mail devotionals, virtual book tours, and more!

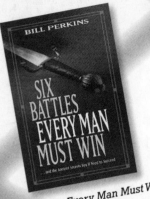